Finding Oasis

Previously published books by Clare Nonhebel

Fiction:
Cold Showers (Betty Trask Award co-winner)
The Partisan
Popcorn, novella in Winter's Tales anthology
Incentives
Child's Play
Eldred Jones, Lulubelle and the Most High

Non-Fiction:
Healed and Souled
Don't Ask Me To Believe
Far From Home
Healing for Life

Finding Oasis

Powerful stories from the slums of Mumbai

Clare Nonhebel

Authentic

16 15 14 13 12 11 10   7 6 5 4 3 2 1

First published 2010 by Authentic Media
Milton Keynes
www.authenticmedia.co.uk

British Library Cataloguing in Publication Data
A catalogue record for this book is available from the British Library

ISBN-13: 978-1-85078-859-1

Cover Design by Rachel Myatt
Printed and bound in Great Britain by Cox and Wyman, Reading

Contents

Contents

Chapter 1

In Suspense

Being suspended thirty-five thousand feet above the earth's surface has the effect of detaching a person from their usual context.

In my case, I'm being detached from the context of UK culture: a multi-ethnic community on the border of Southall in west London, which I hope has gone some way towards preparing me for my destination – Mumbai (or Bombay) in India, where my nephew and his family live. Because John works for a charity, I'll be meeting some of the poorest people in the world, and I'm guessing that nothing in my Western experience has prepared me for that.

I'm not really the adventuring type. In my teens and twenties when many young people go travelling I was struggling with serious illness, and now, half a century old and married to Robin who doesn't like travelling, it doesn't seem the most obvious time to go globe-trotting. My health is fine now but physical stamina is not my strong point and I haven't accumulated the kind of useful skills and work experience that make people in later life helpful to charitable agencies overseas.

Being on my way to India now came about – like many unscheduled events in life – through one of those conversations that don't seem highly significant at the time but keep on repeating themselves in your mind.

I'd attended a seminar at church about mission. The minister challenged everyone to give their 'excuses' for not volunteering for short-term mission.

I didn't need excuses, having a valid reason: I would be useless, a burden. He said he felt the same but added, 'But it's still a cop-out, isn't it? If God calls you, he uses you; it's nothing to do with how useful you think you could be.' A retired missionary confirmed this. 'The only volunteers who were a burden were the ones who thought they knew it all!'

Walking home, I asked God for an indication if he wanted me to do anything. At the same time, I asked him to take me out of any comfort zones I was in.

It felt like one of those dangerous prayers I might later regret, but the answer I heard was not anticipated: 'How comfortable is your life?'

My response was instant and equally unpremeditated: 'It isn't.' It certainly looks like a comfortable life, from the outside. My husband's regular and my sporadic income, several episodes of financial help from living and deceased relatives, and no children of our own, have ensured enough to live on and some to put aside. But the majority of the world's family constantly hunger and thirst, sicken and die, in the backyard of my mind. How can it be comfortable to live comfortably, in such circumstances? How can it be comfortable for any of us, unless we live in denial?

I didn't know if it was a response from God but what came to mind on that walk home was that our nephew John and his Indian wife Charmaine had invited me once to visit them in Bombay, and I hadn't done so.

So I prayed, 'God, if you want me to do this, let them invite me again.' It didn't seem very likely: we rarely saw them.

*   *   *   *

Brought up in Scotland, the youngest of Robin's eldest brother's three children, John went out to Bombay originally for three months, leaving a well-paid graduate job – electronics engineering – in the south-east of England, where he had bought his own home. He went in response to an inner nudge to do something for the poor, who haunted him.

He was part of a three-man team from a UK charity, Oasis Trust, set up by a Baptist minister of British/Indian parentage, Steve Chalke. Oasis set out to empower the poorest and most ignored people to improve their own lives, with whatever help was needed but always including and arising from the workers' own faith in Jesus Christ.

John and the other two stayed with local church families in Bombay, ate what they ate and lived on pocket money while helping out with church projects to reach the unreachable poor – starting with street children. At the end of three months, it didn't seem long enough, so he decided to stay on a bit.

That was fifteen years ago and he never came back, except on visits – alone at first, then for eight months with Charmaine, who is from Bombay, to do a mission course at an international Bible college in the UK, and then on leave, first with one child, then two and now three.

People warned them about the difficulties of cross-cultural marriage, and about trying to 'go native', especially when John was promoted to executive director of

Oasis India. But as Charmaine said, 'At least we're prepared for differences between us; some couples from the
same culture aren't, and find it harder to make adjust-
ments!'And when John's father, Derek, asked one of
John's Indian colleagues if his boss was resented for not
being Indian, the man laughed and said, 'But John is
Indian!'

As a charity worker, John and family return on leave
to the UK every two years. Sometimes we get to see
them when they're here; other years not. The summer I
attended the mission seminar and prayed, they phoned
to say they were near and came for the day. We planned
to take them to the beach – but they brought the monsoon with them! The only day of the summer it rained in
sheets all day.

Around tea-time, John got out the laptop and showed
us photos of Oasis India's projects with street children,
slum dwellers, women trapped in prostitution, people
with HIV and children orphaned by AIDS. I asked a lot
of questions. And he and Charmaine repeated their invitation, 'Come and see.'

I explained I didn't want to come as a tourist, looking
at people as an interesting project. It wasn't as if I could
do anything useful, like build classrooms as another
nephew had just been doing in Brazil.

'Actually,' John said, 'our staff are always being asked
to write about people we've helped, and writing doesn't
come easily to all of us. I was wondering if you'd write
some case histories.' He paused, then added casually,
'And maybe a book.'

*   *   *   *

Telling people I'm going to India has aroused varying
reactions. Some people warn me against the shock of

poverty; others talk poetically about colours, spices and vibrancy of life; those with unfocused spiritual yearnings envisage it as a fount of eastern wisdom, while the materially minded talk about sightseeing, out-of-season suntans and cheap shopping.

I feel so unprepared and unsuitable for this trip, acutely aware of my age, ignorance and tiredness. My shorthand is sometimes slower than longhand and I can't always read it back, and I'll have to rely on interpreters in interviewing Hindi-speakers.

But on the plane I find that what is troubling my mind the most is the culture I've left behind, especially something I read a week ago – a magazine article about life coaching, a growing trend in our Western society's self-fulfilment industry. I don't know why it's nagging at me, on the way to Mumbai, but it is.

The article outlined the starting point of life coaching: inviting the participant to draw a pie-chart of 'my life', dividing it into segments representing elements such as 'my work', 'my ambitions', 'my relationships', and giving each segment a score out of ten for its satisfaction value, then aiming to improve the score in one segment at a time. This seems to me a fragmented and unrealistic view of the rich complexities of life, which is shared with all humanity and can't attain completeness in some individual life plan. It's such a poor alternative to Jesus' offer of 'life in all its fullness' and his purpose for everyone 'to be one, as the Father and I are one.'

I'm wondering whether people born in the very different cultures I'm about to visit – most without knowledge of Jesus but perhaps with more emphasis on life in community rather than 'my life' – rate and react to the stresses of life in the same way.

Are the very poor in India aiming for similar goals to comfortable westerners, and harbouring similar dreams of fulfilling their individual potential? Is the universal longing for peace and happiness experienced and expressed in similar ways, and are the same remedies for human heartache applied in the slums of Mumbai?

And, in such a short visit – eleven days – can a foreigner learn something that may change her own perspective on life?

I'm about to find out.

* * * *

In London, in preparation for the trip, I queued for six hours for a visa outside the Indian High Commission and talked to an Indian man who now had British citizenship and so was also forced to apply for a visa before going back for a visit. He was retired, having first come to England to work in the 1960s. I asked how he had coped with the racism at that time.

He said matter-of-factly that he had lived on a rough estate, had been called names, denied jobs because of his colour, had windows broken in his flat and rubbish pushed through the letterbox. He had finally got a factory job, where he was injured so badly he couldn't return to work for nine months. The first three years had been the worst, he said, before his wife and children could come and join him.

I told him I was sorry he had been treated so badly in our country, and asked why he had stayed – was it worth it?

'Oh yes,' he replied. 'My three sons have all had a good education. The older two have good jobs and the youngest one is at college.'

'Couldn't that have happened in India?' I asked him.

'No. The class system is still very rigid. They wouldn't have had the opportunities.'

I think about him now. All that abuse and being treated like a second-class citizen and he felt satisfied with his choice, and his sacrifice. His purpose was fulfilled, not in his life but in the next generation's lives. I don't think a life-coach would have much to say about that. Who decides what fulfils a life, or even what qualifies as 'my life', distinct from others' lives?

The plane has been losing altitude and now begins circling over Mumbai – a vast undefined cluster of buildings, water and hills studded with lights in the pre-dawn darkness.

For most of the occupants of the plane, this is home. For me, it might as well be another planet. I have everything to learn. I feel that none of the UK-dwelling Asians I know, nothing of the Indian community living on our west London doorstep, nothing I've seen, heard, read or viewed on television, is going to prepare me for this experience.

I have no idea what it will be like. God knows every single life of the millions of people living in this city, is the thought that crosses my mind. He has been the context in which each person has been born and lives and will die. Not a single one takes their first breath or their last breath or any breath during the whole of their life, without him knowing it. Each one is held in the palm of his hand and is rooted in the core of his heart.

And not only in Mumbai but among the billion inhabitants of this Indian subcontinent, from the most opulently wealthy to the heart-crushingly destitute, he knows every single person. And I know five: my Scottish nephew, his Indian wife, and their two little girls and one boy. I can't wait for the plane to land.

Chapter 2

Home from Home

The plane arrives late, having missed its landing slot and risen and circled around and around Mumbai a few more times. It would have been a great overview of the city if it had been light. What I see is enough to show me that it's massive, and that there are more high-rises and also more forests and expanses of water than I had realised. Impenetrable jungle meets impenetrable urban jungle – or that's how it looks from a height and in semi-penetrable light.

Out in the arrivals area there is a sea of faces. I scan the crowd for a white one, and John appears suddenly. We exchange hugs, he seizes the luggage, and I follow him through the crowds. He seems very much at home here.

I didn't quite believe it was going to happen, even while I was having all the injections, queuing for a life-time outside the embassy for a visa stamp on my pass-port, buying supplies of sunscreen and insect repellent and anti-malaria tablets, choosing presents for children I didn't know very well, and for slum children I couldn't imagine.

But it has happened, and I'm here, and as soon as we're outside the airport entrance, two barefooted lit-tle girls with matted hair have come up either side of me, holding their hands out and miming hungry mouths.

I try to explain I have no rupees yet – no money. I was surprised to find out that our local post office, on the borders of one of the biggest Indian communities in Britain, supplied virtually every currency except Indian rupees. I didn't know it was a restricted currency, unavailable outside the country itself.

'But don't worry,' the cashier said with a smile. 'You'll have no trouble changing your money when you arrive. We love sterling!'

These little girls don't love sterling and they don't love me, arriving with my big suitcase and nice clean clothes and not giving them anything. By way of apology, as they don't understand my 'No-rupee,' refrain, I stroke the head of the older girl. She flinches and glares at me. Not on. I say 'Sorry' again. I borrowed a book and a tape of Hindi from the library before I came, but I don't remember anything that might cover this eventuality. *Nahi* – no – seems a bit abrupt. They can hear that anyway.

The drive home from the airport – and from the Oasis India office where John works, which is not far from the airport – can take up to two and a half hours, he warns, depending on traffic. It's early, not seven am yet, so I guess the traffic won't be that bad at this hour. I really do have a lot to learn about Mumbai.

I'm used to London rush hours but London traffic has lanes. Here, there are as many lanes of traffic as there is width of road, so it veers from four to eight without much warning. There are cars that look as though they may fall apart if someone leans against them, exhaling clouds of black exhaust. There are trucks packed with workmen. Motor rickshaws, with passengers keeping their elbows and knees tucked in as they sit in the door-less back seat, nudge their way between other vehicles, with centimetres to spare. Whole families cling to each other on the back of motorbikes, the women riding pillion, sitting sideways and clutching the smallest child, while the older one is sandwiched between the father's arms, holding the handlebars.

Everyone leans on the horn every few minutes, to avoid applying the brakes. After a while I see it's a signalling system, not a sign of annoyance. It's the way a vehicle indicates that it's creating another lane and overtaking, either inside or outside the vehicle just ahead of it. The system seems to work. Schoolchildren try to edge their way across the road and the traffic makes no way for them.

After I return home, John and Charmaine's younger daughter, crossing the road with her sister to go to school, steps out into the traffic and is hit by a truck whose driver has no chance of stopping in time. He runs for his life, not waiting to find out that she will be OK, because he knows onlookers will enforce their own 'justice'. A man comes to tell John, 'We'll find him and beat him for you,' and John has to be very insistent that he is a Christian and doesn't want the man punished: it isn't his fault.

With apparently no street crossings, old ladies in saris, men in business suits – all take their lives in their hands, with no sign of anxiety, and weave their way through the stream of vehicles. The traffic only slows down for cows, and sometimes for red traffic lights.

I wasn't expecting the cows, somehow – not in the city itself, alongside the main arterial roads. I thought a few might linger on the outskirts, where the city peters out into countryside or at least suburbs. But all forms of life are here. Everywhere. I have never seen so many people. So many stray dogs. Cows, goats, chickens. All living by the roadside.

And the children. The road is tarmac laid on a base of hardcore as most major roads are, all over the world. You can see the layers of the road surface as they drop down into soil and stone by the roadside.

'No pavements,' I comment.

'There are in some places,' John says, 'but people tend to put up stalls on them, so everyone still walks on the road.'

There is a constant stream of people walking along the road. The women are dressed in saris or, mostly, in *shalwar kameez* – the long tunic, full trousers narrowed at the ankle or from the calf, and a long gauzy *dupatta* scarf. The colours are beautiful. Most of the women have long hair, tied back or up, many with ornaments. The men wear shirts and trousers or shorts, or tunics and trousers or, a few, a *dhoti* – a kind of draped shorts-cum-skirt. Unlike London commuters, most are not carrying bags, briefcases or anything.

People are living on the roadside. Children are sleeping and waking up, being washed from a bucket, being dressed, having a drink, on the level of the constant cloud of black exhaust fumes. People are cleaning their teeth beside the road. Every private function has to be performed in public, witnessed by the stream of commuters in their various vehicles. People have been sleeping on shop-fronts, small individual shops. I don't know what I expected. Tesco?

Roadworks appear suddenly in the road, with a tape around the chasm but no advance warning. All the lanes converge to avoid the hole. Horns sound a whole symphony. Some drivers even apply brakes.

'Is a horn more essential to driving than brakes here?' I ask John.

He laughs. 'I must admit, the horn on my last car failed once and I felt very vulnerable till it was fixed!'

He gives me facts about Bombay. Both he and
Charmaine still call it Bombay, not Mumbai. One of his
uncles in England keeps asking when he's going to come
home but it's quite clear that he is at home in this city.
Bombay is an island, he says. Water surrounds it and
there are lakes and forests in the middle. In Thane (pro-
nounced Tahn-eh) on the outskirts, where the family
lives, as well as high-rise estates there are forested hills
with tribal villages, with people living as they have
always lived. Some of the village houses are rudimentary shelters, some are made of sticks and cattle dung,
while others have been rebuilt in block or brick.

There are crocodiles in the lakes and leopards in the
hills. In the evenings sometimes the leopards come
down to the city, hungry. Mostly they prey on the stray
dogs, which sleep on the roadsides by day but gather
into packs in the evenings and go scavenging. A few
months ago, John says, a leopard took a small boy from
outside a block of flats on the edge of town.

Jungle and urban jungle overlap then, at times. I wonder which is scarier, a leopard in the suburbs of Mumbai
or a knife-wielding mugger in a London subway?

People are so close together, whether walking along,
driving, or living. A friend from Sri Lanka told me that
people from the subcontinent don't have the same concept of personal space that British people have. She had
to learn, in coming to the UK, that if you get on a bus
and there's only one person sitting on it, you sit far
away. If there are two individuals, you divide the space
between them and choose a seat there. In Sri Lanka this
would be considered rude, unfriendly and odd. You
would be expected to sit next to the person who was
there first, or at least greet them and speak a few words.
Here, people walk very close to each other and don't
seem to object to being jostled in the general progress.

The drivers also show no sign of the road rage I've grown accustomed to in London. The horn-blowing here is a function of driving, not a form of swearing.

'How many people are there living here?' I ask.

'Officially, the population of Bombay is under ten million,' John says.

'And unofficially?'

'Probably nearer twenty million. About six million travel across Bombay on the railway every day; there are two main lines through the city.'

A few months after my return to the UK, a terrorist gang will plant seven bombs on local Mumbai trains which explode in rush-hour time, killing and maiming many. Longer-term damage is caused, I'm told later, to many people's hearing – both those who were on the trains and those who live in the vicinity.

'You'll get to see some of the stations,' John says. 'There are about one hundred thousand children living on the railway platforms and on the streets around the stations. They used to be mainly on Thane station but they've moved away now.'

'Why?'

He shrugs. 'It's the nature of a moving population to keep moving. Oasis has had to move with them. The street children's drop-in centre has gone from Thane station and we've set up in another area now. Charmaine and I are thinking of moving house, further into the city. The street children were our original reason for coming to Thane.'

Everyone I see is thin. Weight Watchers wouldn't do well here. But I realise that my preconceived idea of people living below the poverty line is of passivity. Maybe most westerners have that idea, from TV documentaries on famine where people are shown sitting hopelessly waiting for handouts after a crisis. People here are obviously

extremely poor but they are not passive; they seem motivated and resourceful. I can't imagine, if I had slept all
night by the main road, bombarded with noise and mosquitoes and inhaling petrol exhaust, that I would get up
and bother to brush my teeth in the morning and dress
neatly and walk miles to work, if necessary.

'We don't realise we have prejudices till we're con-
fronted with them,' I suggest.

'It helps to live in another culture,' John says. 'What I
tell all the visitors and volunteers who come out here is,
don't compare it with home.'

I can see the point, and the mistake other cultures
make by imposing their own solutions, devised from
their world-view, on a society which has different norms
and which, if it were consulted, would provide more
workable solutions of its own. But it's hard not to compare. If this poverty and overcrowding existed in the
UK, people would be raging against Social Services or
threatening to bring down the government.

We're passing the lakes and hills now, thickly forested
and looking somehow untouched, though right by the
busy city. Much of the land in Bombay, John says, is still
owned by tribal communities. Buying a plot can be complicated when it has common ownership among a whole
tribe and every person in it has to agree to its being sold.
It isn't an issue in the estate where the family lives, an
enclosed area of tall apartment blocks with a playground in the grounds – for use in the early evenings
when it isn't too hot for the children to play outside.

There are security guards on the gates, looking bored
as cars drive in and out. Beyond the car park there is a
stretch of open ground leading to an estate of another
kind, a settlement of low self-built shelters and houses,
with a toilet block in a field and people hanging out

washing and wandering about. A volleyball net is set up in the car park.

Inside the open foyer of the apartment building another security guard sits. The names of all the apartments' occupants are listed on the wall. John and Charmaine's flat is in Charmaine's name, as non-Indians are not allowed to own property and John still has British nationality.

'But she lets me live here rent-free!' he jokes.

He calls the lift to go up to the seventh floor where they live.

All the apartments have double front doors – an outer security door with a metal grille that covers the glass pane in the inner door. Most apartments have both doors open now, as children are leaving for school. Inside, ceiling fans whirr. It's only February so it's cool by Mumbai standards now. But my body is adapted to English February and it seems very hot to me.

We have breakfast and Charmaine shows me round the flat and explains the water filtration unit over the kitchen sink: 'Don't drink water from the tap, only from these jugs once it's been filtered.' The milk is boiled and left to cool in jugs – unsafe to drink in its raw state too, because of the risk of TB.

Charmaine met John when she was working with street children. A boy living on the railway platform fell sick and Charmaine, recognising a passing charity worker by his Oasis T-shirt, asked him to help with getting the boy admitted to hospital. On rickshaw journeys to and from the hospital, they had a chance to get to know each other and discovered they shared a concern for the poorest members of society, as well as a strong personal faith and a sense of humour based on appreciating the ridiculous.

John has a meeting at Oasis's vocational training centre this afternoon and suggests I have a sleep now to make up for the missed night, then go with him and meet some of the people there. This is what I've come for, to see the projects, interview people and write case histories, as an aid to raising awareness of the charity's work. I still feel painfully aware of my limitations. I feel middle-aged and English, likely to offend people by my ignorance of their culture, by my background, my clothes and my lack of tact. I'm imposing on this busy young family, possibly for no useful benefit.

But at least I got here. So the first stage went OK.

The ceiling fans go off and there is a high-pitched singing noise in the background.

'It's the generator starting up,' Charmaine explains. 'There are power cuts from eight-thirty to eleven-thirty every morning. In some parts of Bombay the power goes off for longer. There isn't enough to go round. The water goes off sometimes too, but at odd times; we don't know when it's going to happen.'

I decide to use the water while it's available and have a shower. The cold water is refreshing.

I turn back the beautiful elephant-printed cotton cover, which is the only bedding necessary in this hot climate, and peace settles suddenly.

Iain, left to himself now his older sisters have gone to school, is playing and chatting to himself in the corridor. From the window, I can see people walking across open ground from the village houses.

I can't remember why I had any doubts. I get the feeling this visit is going to be good.

Chapter 3

In Training

When I wake up, Charmaine introduces me to the two
maids who come in to help with the cleaning and household chores, Gaudi and Joshan. They sit cross-legged on
the floor, eating their lunch. They're not comfortable
with sitting up at the table to eat, although Charmaine
invites them. In this part of the world where too many
people search after too little work, it makes sense for
many hands to make light work in homes like this where
a family is privileged to have a home and a wage-
earner. To Western minds it may seem odd for a charity
worker to employ domestic help, but charity begins at
home.

Gaudi and Charmaine work alongside each other
smoothly, sharing the chores and chatting about family.
Joshan comes to help out in the morning and returns in
the evening to take Iain down to the playground, leaving Charmaine free to concentrate on helping the girls
with homework.

Schools rely heavily on parents to ensure children
have absorbed the day's lessons at school. Classes are
large – up to eighty pupils, much of the material is mem-
orised and recited, and workbooks are used to keep the
children focused and occupied. Schooling is technically
free for every child, though Charmaine explains there

are hidden expenses: registration fees, books and uniforms in some cases, so some parents still can't afford to send children to school, which are in any case hard-pushed to accommodate those who can go.

Typically, schools work two shifts a day, with some children starting in the morning and coming home in early afternoon, and the second shift running in the afternoon. Sending children to a school that charges fees may guarantee smaller classes – between thirty and forty – but a place even at primary school is not guaranteed; they are simply oversubscribed.

We eat lunch, which is delicious – spicy vegetable mixtures, salad, and fresh bread that is chewy and light at the same time. Charmaine promises to introduce me to various dishes while I'm here, but warns me not to eat salad or *raita*, a milky sauce with raw vegetables in it, while I'm out. If vegetables haven't been washed in purified water, they're risky for visitors.

When it's time to leave for the training centre in town, the electrical power has been resumed and Iain is able to watch his video of the BBC children's programme *Balamory* – unknown on Indian television but beloved by all three children because their cousins live in the Scottish island town where it is set.

On the way to the training centre, I see some obvious slums and some prosperous-looking office tower blocks. I ask which are the upmarket areas and which are the slum areas of Mumbai, and John says, 'It's not like that. Bombay is fifty-one percent slum, and the slums are in every area. The developers are always wanting to knock them down because some are on prime building land. You'll get to go into some slums.'

A new part of the highway is being built and the traffic slows long enough to allow a chance to watch the road-building team. They are the thinnest people I have yet seen, like matchstick men and women, carrying loads of rock on their heads and walking barefoot over rubble. In the distance is one small excavator grubbing up the rocky ground. It is the only piece of machinery. There is not even a wheelbarrow. Children are also working, following their parents and carrying heavy rocks in their arms. It looks exhausting. Behind the stretch of ground they are working on are the families' living quarters: tents fabricated from tree branches and plastic sheeting or sheets of rusty corrugated iron.

'Where do they get water?' I ask John.

'They probably have to walk quite a long way for it – but if they'd stayed in the villages, it would be six or seven kilometres. That's why so many people move into the city.'

Even in the shopping and business areas, I see very few advertising hoardings, and these do no more than advertise the product. I've grown used, in London, to the huge images of half-naked women and men, the double-meaning slogans and sexually explicit messages. No wonder visitors from overseas are shocked and offended by us. I thought Bombay, as the cradle of Bollywood movies, would be more overtly erotic in its culture.

We drive past one of the red-light districts. John indicates the girls waiting outside the shop-fronts, and others sitting in rooms above the shops, behind the window bars. The girls look very young, very sad and lifeless.

'They're so respectably dressed!' I'm surprised. They are dressed like everyone else, in saris or *shalwar kameez*, with neatly tied long hair. I think of the prostitutes in Soho in central London, by the roadside in Rome or in hotels in the Middle East. There are no hoardings outside the brothels here, no lurid images of women licking their lips, clad in leather mini-skirts, thongs and thigh-boots, or cracking whips and snarling.

It dawns on me why. In present day British culture, sex is regarded as a game, a fun part of an active social life, a dare, a tease, a laugh, a status symbol. It's marketed as part of the leisure industry, with the glamour of entertainment. Here, it is life and death. It is deadly serious business.

'Most of these girls have been trafficked,' John says. 'They're sold into the trade and kept here as slaves. In one area they're actually kept behind bars, in cages, with customers looking in at them.'

'What's being done to stop the trafficking?'

'Various agencies are trying, including Oasis. We've been working with the police in Bangalore, designing computer programs to connect all the police departments round the country in reporting and tracking missing women and children. We've been asked by the Child Welfare staff in Bangalore if we can help care for the people who have been trafficked; once the police have got them out, there's nowhere to put them. The children are housed in remand homes which are terribly overcrowded. Skin infections, for instance, spread like wildfire because the children are sleeping side by side on the floor, packed in like sardines. Also, there have been problems with security. Some children have been taken from the homes and retrafficked.'

'If the children were abducted, can't they go home again once they've been traced?'

'Some do – the ones whose parents have reported them missing. But a lot are never claimed, and once they're eighteen, they're not legally the government's responsibility.'

'Is it all for prostitution, the trafficking?'

'No, some of it's for child labour. That's why so many end up in Bangalore; they're sold to the factories there.

But there's also the child sex trade, of course. Some just disappear.'

'On what sort of scale is this going on?'

'We don't know. Hundreds of thousands certainly, but that's probably the tip of the iceberg. Oasis is part of a campaign called *Stop The Traffik* which hopefully will make people more aware. It's worse now than the slave trade that William Wilberforce campaigned against in the 1800s.'

They look so alone, these young girls.

'What a nightmare! Do you succeed in getting many of them out?'

'You're about to meet some of them at the Vocational Training Centre. Women who leave the trade come to our halfway house for counselling and health care, then when they're ready we offer them training in tailoring or other skills.'

'How do you get to meet them? Aren't they wary of strangers approaching them?'

'The drop-in centre has helped. You can go there tomorrow if you'd like to. The girls come in for health care or literacy classes or just to chat to someone. And the girls on our staff are beginning to be allowed to go into the brothels and talk to them.'

'The madams let them go in and talk to the prostitutes and offer them help to get out of the trade? How come they allow that?'

'I guess it's God's grace. The staff try and build up relationships with everybody – the madams, the pimps, the girls. They are suspicious at first, obviously. But they have their own histories; they need friendship as well.'

It seems a stupendous task, given the scale of need. Looking at the vast areas of slums, thinking of the huge numbers of children sold into slavery and the poor young women forced into prostitution, it must seem so dispiriting, so pointless even to try to oppose the very determined forces behind this dark industry feeding on people's poverty and vulnerability. How do they find the motivation, the people at Oasis and the other charities who chip away patiently at the foundations of greed and emotional damage that sustain this horrific empire of discarded people?

I'm about to ask John but I see he's just answered it. It has to be the grace of God. Who else could supply the sheer perseverance and courage?

The car turns down a road by a dusty patch of soil outside a row of apartment blocks, where some schoolboys are playing cricket. At the end of the road is a two-storey block which looks unfinished, with a corrugated iron canopy where the roof or the next storey might be, and open, doorless rooms. Upstairs, bright curtains hang from metal bars tied to the scaffolding uprights.

A group of teenage boys in T-shirts and jeans, most barefoot, are working in one of the downstairs rooms, clearly a workshop. They say hello and pause for a minute before carrying on with their work.

John leads the way into a small office crammed with chairs awaiting the people who'll come to the meeting. While people are being summoned from other parts of the building, I meet Sanjiv, one of the project leaders, and ask him about the boys in the workshop. How easy is it for street boys to adapt to the kind of industrious concentration that these are displaying?

'They start with a lot of fears,' says Sanjiv, 'and some refuse to accept help because of it. There's fear of accountability: "Someone expects something of me; what if I can't do it?" Then, they're not in control of their own lives here. On the street they have the freedom to make their own decisions, and no discipline. Many would rather sleep on the street or under a bridge than in a room where lights are switched off at 10.30. They've run away from poverty or from parents, then they run away from responsibility or accountability. Authority has been misused in their lives, so it's feared.'

At this point the other staff members come into the office for the meeting, among them some of the trainers at the centre and a trainer from Oasis's centre in Bangalore, an English lady called Brenda. John tells her I'll meet her again as we're going to go to Bangalore next week. I didn't know this was on the itinerary and it sounds an exciting opportunity.

There isn't time to talk to her now as the meeting is about to begin. John introduces me to Saby, who has offered to show me round the centre, and we go and sit outside while he explains how it operates.

Saby and his family were house-parents of the home for street boys set up as one of Oasis India's earliest projects in 1994, caring for eight boys between the ages of seventeen and twenty-two. A training facility for them and for women from the streets was envisaged from the beginning, with referrals coming from non-governmental organisations, churches, other charities, and boys' homes.

Training initially took the form of a one-year tailoring course, chosen to suit women as well as men because tailoring work can be done at home and there is a cultural restriction on women living with parents: they are allowed to study but not to get jobs outside the home. Tailoring training is still offered, to both sexes, along with a one-year course in electrical work and screen-printing – the boys do six months of each. They also receive tuition in literacy, numeracy, Hindi, English and IT, as part of the National Open School curriculum which takes students up to Tenth Standard of the Indian school system – preparation for college.

Women who do well on the tailoring course can also do embroidery and, a recent addition, Aari work – a bead and sequin-embellished form of embroidery worked on a raised frame like a bed-frame which holds the fabric taut while the embroiderers sit on the floor and sew through it.

Once Oasis found which skills were manageable and marketable, they extended the same patterns of tuition to their other projects, so I will see the same activities going on in the slum communities and the centre for women and children with HIV/AIDS. They are also offered in other cities – Oasis India works in Bangalore and Chennai (formerly called Madras) as well as in Mumbai. Life skills are also taught – topics such as family, self-esteem, cleanliness, health issues including HIV and other subjects that young people with no family or home have no way of learning.

'They have a short attention span,' Saby says. 'If they've had no education, it's hard for them to understand. Everything has to be illustrated. They ask a lot of questions, trying to relate it to their experience.'

Counselling is on-going, with every manager, carer or tutor trained and willing to listen whenever anyone needs to talk. The lives of people coming into these projects have been traumatic; it doesn't come easily to them to trust anyone, so when they do want to talk it's important that someone makes time for them.

The boys hover round while Saby is talking, and he invites them to demonstrate their screen-printing skills, which they do solemnly and with attention. They are keener to have their photos taken, though, and to see the images on my digital camera screen.

One boy, already taller than the others, runs to fetch his stilts and demonstrates his stilt-walking expertise, and at this the serious expressions of all of them break into grins and two more faces appear, laughing, between the curtains shading the upper storey.

Saby asks the boys if any of them are willing to tell me their story, and most melt away at this point except one younger boy. Saby tells him we'll come back to him; we're going to see round the centre first. The boy looks nervous and I tell him he can just tell me what he wants; there's no need to answer any questions he doesn't want to. He nods and goes back to work.

Saby introduces some of the tutors. There are eight to ten staff at the centre, some part-time. An IT consultant comes once a week and IT skills are taught to everyone, along with their chosen course, to empower those with none of life's advantages to keep up in a computer-reliant society.

Trainees receive a stipend of forty rupees a day (about 55p) plus travel costs and a train pass, a cooked meal for twelve rupees (free to the residential boys) and morning and afternoon *chai* – the regular form of tea brewed with hot milk and sugar, sometimes flavoured with spices.

The centre accommodates a surprising number of activities in a relatively small space, and the work the students display is good. The overall impression of the place is homeliness. With bare floors and only the most basic furnishings, the friendliness and humour among students and staff create a relaxed atmosphere. This is a community that thrives on prayer, with informal times of sharing and also more structured worship meetings which the staff take turns to lead.

I talk to Liz, who has worked as a teacher here for five years, her first job after college, and she says faith in God is intrinsic to her work. 'God has dealt with me first,' she admits. 'Patience is one thing I had to learn. You don't feel like loving the people here always but God puts a love for them into your heart.'

Boys and girls are taught separately. There are currently ten trainees; four have dropped out. One of the boys has just left.

'They get emotional breakdowns and lose courage,' Liz explains, 'and at the last moment they say, "I'm not doing the exam!" I've learned not to get let down; God is doing something different. It takes a lot of time for someone to share about themselves and how they feel. We don't expect a lot from them. Then, as we build up the relationship, they gain confidence and see they can do more.'

'What about their own expectations?' I ask. 'What are their dreams?'

'Most want to learn something new,' Liz says, 'and to learn English and set up their own business.'

She introduces me to two of the tailoring students, Padma and Sasthi, who have done eight months of their course, and they demonstrate their pattern-cutting skills. I tell them I've only ever used printed dressmaking patterns and find that quite complicated.

A couple of former trainees are now employed here, training others. The dividing line between staff and beneficiaries (recipients of the charity's services) is blurred here, as at all the Oasis projects.

Some newcomers to the Vocational Training Centre find it strange to encounter the prayer dimension of such a practical environment but Saby says most of the young people like it, especially the annual retreat.'They like being together for a longer time. We have fun: picnics, drama sketches, dressing up, and we have outside speakers come and talk.'

It's part of the preparation for independent life, as the residential boys only attend the centre for two years, one for training and one for employment.

Sharing faith in Jesus Christ is controversial in Indian society, which officially tolerates all religions but which includes Hindu fundamentalists who deeply resent Christianity. Western evangelistic mission organisations are illegal. The charity needs its supporters who pray for the protection of workers and beneficiaries; they can't take personal safety for granted. There will always also be people, of other religions or none – or even other Christians – who accuse Christian workers of taking advantage of the vulnerable people who accept material help, by sharing with them a gospel they neither know nor have invited. But how could any worker, having experienced the incredible privilege of knowing Jesus Christ, withhold it from a woman who has been sold and exploited, or a street child who has no home?

No one has to take part in prayer times, but most can relate to the God who sent his Son to share the life of outcasts and who offers unconditional love, not condemnation, and a way out of darkness into a new innocence.

After training, women who want to set up their own tailoring businesses are given free use of the Centre's facilities and equipment for a year, keeping the money from the garments they sell. It's a confidence boost as well as financial support: it's a big step to go self-employed – for anyone, let alone those who have come up from the streets.

A three-person reintegration team helps students who have completed courses to move on and find jobs and somewhere to live. Saby is about to head this team, easing the interim period between care and independence.

'Three boys are living together in their own home now,' says Saby. 'Oasis gives the deposit and helps them get started; the following year they'll be independent. They're invited to all our meetings and we visit them, and we introduce them to local pastors so the church will keep an eye on them and give them support.'

There's no pressure on the boys to attend church, nor to remain in touch with Oasis after they've left, but several of the staff comment that those who develop their own personal faith in Christ cope better and grow in maturity, showing less dependence on staff and more emotional stability.

I'm looking forward to interviewing a few in the coming days – both the current students here and those who have moved on, some now employed by Oasis helping other young people to leave the streets, the poverty of the slum or the trap of prostitution.

It's a privilege to be allowed to meet them and ask them questions about their lives – if they're willing to talk to me. I don't see why anyone would be willing to tell some stranger from a cushier part of the world where home and care and education are taken for granted and regarded as a right, about their humiliations and trials.

I hope that some will, because I want to learn what it's like to live their lives – to hear it in their own words and see it in their eyes. I've read case studies and newspaper articles, as we all have, and watched documentaries on issues such as street children, prostitution and world poverty. But these people who are here now, quietly sewing or printing or tapping computer keyboards, are not issues. They are unique individuals carrying a history that has stacked all the odds against them being here right now, having survived.

Chapter 4

Childhood Lost and Found

Smita, head of tailoring, has volunteered to interpret for Sanam, one of the young girl trainees. We sit outside on the step, out of earshot of the boys. Sanam is shy and keeps her head down, stealing quick sideways glances as I ask her questions, then looking at Smita to translate her replies. She has agreed to let her story be known, but telling it is obviously not easy. Smita fills in some of the gaps for her.

Sanam doesn't know her date of birth or her exact age, Smita explains. The staff have estimated that she is nineteen. All Sanam knows is that her childhood ended abruptly at the age of seven or eight, when her aunt sold her to a 'dance bar' where she was forced to work until rescued by a charity called IJM (International Justice Mission) and referred to Oasis. She came to live in Oasis' halfway home for women and girls and, when ready, began vocational training here at the Centre.

I ask Sanam if she will tell me how she felt, and she begins falteringly but with determination.

'I was waiting for someone to come and help me, to rescue me,' she says.

'What was your dream?' I ask her.

'I wanted to get an education and to learn tailoring.'

It seems a painfully reasonable dream. I wonder how many British teenage girls dream of getting an education.

Probably more dream of getting out of it as soon as possible, seeing education as a short-term denial of freedom rather than a route to freedom.

'Did you think your dream would happen?' I ask, and she shakes her head.

'No. At first there seemed no chance of getting what I wanted. From childhood, I never expected love. I wanted it but I couldn't expect it.'

'Did it seem real to you, when people wanted to help you? Did you believe it was genuine?'

'It was hard to believe,' she says. 'Hard to accept love. I thought, "Is it true or not?" It took me a long time to trust.'

'When did you realise it was for real?' I ask.

'I couldn't believe it!' she says, looking up for the first time and speaking with animation in her voice. 'I couldn't believe, when I was rescued from the area. Two or three people kept coming back to see me. They said they would rescue me, but it actually happened!'

Sanam becomes emotional here. I move on to an easier topic and ask about her plans for the future.

'I'm doing the tailoring training and I can think about the next step,' she says.

'What would you like, as your next step?'

'I'd like to work in a factory, or perhaps become a teacher, teaching tailoring. What I'd like most is to be like Smita.' Sanam gives a sideways glance at Smita, who laughs.

Sanam is not used to talking about herself, it's clear, and she is starting to fidget and look back at the door she has come through. I scribble down the last shorthand outline hurriedly and thank her for sharing her story. She smiles, then hesitates.

'Is there anything else you'd like to say?' I ask her and she nods – the swift left-right-up-down Indian nod of the head that I haven't learned quite to differentiate from a head shake. I take it as a yes, and wait. She clenches her hands, and speaks with deliberate confidence.

'I'm a different person now,' Sanam says. 'I can think about the future. There are people who love me.'

She stands up, looking at Smita, and asks her a question.

'Sanam wants to know, is that enough?' Smita asks me.

'Please tell her it's wonderful,' I say, 'and thank her very much.'

Sanam smiles suddenly, and she and Smita stand and exchange a few words as Saby reappears and calls out that he'll be back in a minute with Pranad, the young boy.

Sanam points at the place where I'm standing and says something to Smita, who looks in the same direction.

'Your feet!' Smita says. 'They are swollen.'

I look down and find I have elephant feet. I hadn't noticed. Having asked Charmaine's advice, I'd changed out of my just-below-knee-length summer dress which would not be regarded as decent for a grown woman here, and put on the one long skirt I possess. Hitching it up slightly, I see I have elephant ankles to match. It must be from the flight, though I did wear flight socks for all but the final descent. Or maybe it's the heat.

What surprises me is Sanam's concern. How can a girl sold into slavery, who spent her entire childhood and young life being brutalised, spare a concern for some foreign middle-aged woman with a minor ailment? I have a sudden urge to cry, and am glad to be distracted by Smita sitting down and starting to talk, as Sanam goes back to work.

'When Sanam first came here, she wouldn't speak at all,' Smita tells me. 'She's been living in the halfway house about a year now. Everyone here has a difficult background. One of the boys, Samarjit, is a prostitute's son, and Padma is an orphan. She has two brothers and no financial support.

'I was a trainee here, in tailoring, then I joined as assistant teacher and now I'm head of the unit. I'm a pastor's daughter. I failed Tenth Standard at school. My language is Marathi[1] but the final exams were in Hindi.

'When I first came here I used to get so upset. I wanted to earn the girls' trust so they could come to me for guidance or love, but I didn't know how to be positive. And my mum didn't want me teaching or eating with people who had HIV. But I gave her information about it, and I just prayed for God's grace. I felt I could cry when I heard the stories of people's lives.'

I'm beginning to know how she felt. 'How do you cope with it, day after day?'

She smiles. 'God's grace,' she says.

Saby is here now, with Pranad. Smita gets up and goes back to teaching her trainees. Pranad is slightly embarrassed, aware of being watched from a distance by the other boys. I explain that I want to write about the lives of people here so that people in my country and others, who have much easier lives, will read it and understand.

'Tell us what it's like to be you. And tell us what you think we need to learn.'

He nods but looks anxiously at Saby.

'He's worried that his English isn't good enough,' Saby explains, 'but I've told him I'll translate for him.'

Encouraged, Pranad begins. 'I am sixteen years old,' he begins, 'and I have three names.' He tells me them. They are long and I need help to spell them. It's a lot of name for one young boy.

'They are all names of Hindu gods,' Saby explains.

Apart from the auspicious names, Pranad's family wasn't able to give him much to set him up in life.

'I come from Andhra Pradesh,' he says. 'I used to live with my family in a village but the family was very poor so I came with my aunty to the city near my home. She brought me there to work for one year, in a house. Then I moved to Bombay.'

'A lot of boys come here,' says Saby. 'Either they run away from home or there's no work for them there, so they come to the city.'

'It was four days by train,' Pranad continues. 'And two changes of train.'

'How old were you then?'

'I was twelve or thirteen. I didn't know Hindi, or Marathi. My mother tongue was Telgu. I came out of the station with no job and no way to speak to anyone. So I lived on the station, on the platform.'

'What was that like for you?' I ask.

'I did jobs, but sometimes there were no jobs,' Pranad says.

'What jobs did you do?'

'I used to be a porter, for tips, or sweep the train compartments.' He hesitates. 'My friend and I, we did some work for the police sometimes.'

'For the police?'

'Yes.'

'What did you do for the police, Pranad?'

He has gone very serious. I am suddenly not sure I want to know.

'When there was an accident on the track,' he says, 'we had to carry the dead bodies off the line. The police paid us 150 rupees[2] to carry one dead body.'

Twelve years old. What are our twelve-year-olds doing? Playing football and computer games. Riding bikes. Getting into trouble, perhaps. But . . . carrying smashed-up corpses off the railway line, in order to earn enough to stay alive?

'Was that the worst thing?' I ask Pranad.

'No.'

'What was the worst thing? You don't have to answer any question you don't want to,' I add quickly. What right do I have to ask this sixteen-year-old what he had to do in order to survive?

'The worst thing, when I was living on the platform, was when there were no jobs and I had to go hungry.'

'How long did you live on the station, Pranad?'

He isn't sure. 'I moved on after a while. I got my own business,' he says proudly. 'I sold lime juice on the road-side.'

I've seen the barrows with their piles of limes or other fruit, ready to be squeezed into cups and diluted with water and sold to thirsty commuters on the walk home.

'But I fell sick and I couldn't work. I lost the business and I was back on the platform.'

His voice sinks low. I picture the proud businessman with his barrow of limes, then the return to square one, a homeless street boy again.

'Then my friend and I worked for a wedding store, living together in a home owned by the owners. We got 150 rupees per wedding, decorating the hall. But then, with others, I got addicted to drink and I lost the job. Then I worked in a theatre and got a small rented place to live, together with friends. But I fell sick again and I was back to living on the station.'

'How old were you by then?'

'I was nearly fourteen. That's when I met the Oasis staff. For one year I went to Ashadeep[3] and then I came to the Training Centre.'

'You like it here?'

'Yes. I like all the activities here. And I came to know the Lord,' Pranad says, 'and I felt my life could be much better. I pray for my family. I always remembered my family and I've been back home once or twice.'

'And what would you like for the future, Pranad? Do you have a dream?'

'Yes,' he says. 'I have a dream. When I get a proper job I want to give the money to my family.'

I thank him for his time and go indoors with Saby. The staff have finished their meeting and it's nearly time to go.

If I'm going to keep doing these interviews, I can't afford to dwell on what people are telling me. I'll just have to concentrate on listening and getting the words down accurately, hoping I'll be able to read back my shorthand when I get home. And then I can afford to let it sink in, about the lives that these children have lived. If I stop to think about it now, I'll start crying. And then I won't be any use to anybody.

Chapter 5

Searching for Oasis

Friday morning is the monthly meeting of Oasis India staff. John tells me that as many staff as possible attend, from the cities of Bangalore and Chennai as well as from Mumbai, with an opportunity being given to the newest staff members to experience being part of the organisation. He suggests that I come along and, instead of attending the meeting, take people aside one at a time and interview them to get an overview of the different projects and the people who work on them. It sounds a good idea.

The meeting is held in borrowed premises – a Methodist church – as the Oasis main office is too small to accommodate so many people. There seem to be about sixty people present when we arrive, and the sound of singing greets us from the car park.

'We start the meetings with prayer,' John explains. That's no surprise: most Christian organisations start and finish their business meetings with a prayer. What John omits to mention is that Oasis' monthly meeting starts with two hours of prayer, complete with singing and praising, Bible teaching, and a full-length sermon! It's a clear indication of the charity's priorities and the fuel on which all its enterprise runs. Without constant reliance on God, individually and as a community, there's no way that anyone could do this kind of work without getting either hardened or burnt out.

The sermon will be given by a pastor who is not attached to this particular church but has become involved with Oasis. I've heard of him already – he has started a church for prostitutes in one of the central red-light districts of Mumbai. I wonder what he's like and imagine some dynamic Indian version of the classic American televangelist. I hope he won't shout when he's preaching. If this Pastor Thomas is the go-get-'em type – and presumably he is, doing ground-breaking work in city red-light districts – then I fully expect to emerge from the prayer service feeling more useless, discouraged and selfish than when I went in. Motivational sermons usually have that effect.

I didn't expect so many staff members, in a street-level charity that has only been going for fifteen years. There are now over a hundred staff covering nineteen projects in three cities. Some of the people here are chatting animatedly; others look less confident. Small groups continue to arrive as the ones already in the church get into the singing and worship.

It's in English, I'm relieved to find, and people's accents are understandable. Many of the staff seem quite young, early twenties; others are older. It is quite a varied bunch.

Several people stand up and talk but no one seems to be a pastor. A break is announced and everyone goes outside for a chat in the bright sunshine and a little disposable cup of *chai*. It is flavoured with something I can't identify which Charmaine tells me later is probably cardamom.

The staff are friendly and introduce themselves and each other. I meet Archana, a girl in her twenties, and her colleague Das, a man of about the same age, who run the Ashadeep project – the drop-in centre and outreach work to street children. Ashadeep has moved recently, from Thane station near where John and Charmaine and family live to the vicinity of Kurla station and VT – Victoria Terminus – the main central station, where more of the homeless children now go.

'That's where most of the children arrive, from North India, Bihar and UP,'⁴ Archana explains. 'Contractors pick them up and put them to work, rag-picking, sewing or working in restaurants – illegal child-labour.'

'Do the police do anything?'

'No. They harass the teenage children and beat them, then if we try to help, the police say they steal and harass people and we are encouraging them. If a child is injured, the police give them one hundred rupees for medication but it's to make them go away and not complain; they know the child will spend it on sniffing solvent.'

Someone comes up and greets her and she turns to say hello.

'Perhaps I could talk to you more about your work, sometime this morning?' I ask before she moves away.

'No,' she says firmly. 'You must come and see the project for yourself. Has John arranged for you to visit us?'

'I don't know.'

'Tell him to phone me and say what day you will come,' she says.

'OK.' I'm glad to see she's not in awe of the boss.

A couple of older ladies come over. They work in one of the slum communities, teaching the pre-school children. The children learn the letters of the Hindi alphabet, sing songs, draw pictures and learn about hygiene – skills such as using the toilet and washing their hands, and the reasons for keeping clean. Such knowledge could mean survival for them and their families in an environment with so many hazards to health.

Several people say I should visit Purnata Bhavan (House of Wholeness) the home for women and children affected by HIV and AIDS, which is a couple of hours' drive out of the city. Then there's Aruna, the drop-in centre and outreach work for prostitutes; the visit there is already arranged, for this afternoon. I'd like to see everything but it doesn't make sense to spread the time too thin.

John appears and says, 'Come and meet Pastor Thomas.' I prepare to meet this giant-for-Christ and find instead a thin man with a gentle face, who looks shy. He shakes hands and asks politely about my books, and I ask about his work with the prostitutes. Instead, he talks about Oasis and the work they are doing, and how pleased he is to be part of it.

I don't think he will shout in church.

Later I hear that up to fifteen girls a week are coming to the Sunday service in the red-light district, and this year twelve have made the decision to leave prostitution. In a trade where girls are trafficked and deprived of all choice from the age of twelve or even younger, deciding to accept help when it is finally offered requires courage and trust.

Many girls have been sold then 'rescued' by traffickers and resold to another brothel for a higher profit. So in deciding to accept the help of kind people who are offering them – again – a better life somewhere else, the girls are taking a new risk and facing the unknown. For many, it must seem safer to stay where they are, however abusive the environment.

People are starting to move back into the building. I ask Thomas quickly, 'How do you get prostitutes to go to church?'

'I had the idea for some time that this was needed,' he says. 'Then I heard Oasis was working in this area and I thought we could co-operate.'

It's not a very revealing answer but then there isn't very much time. We go back inside and after some more songs and praise, the pastor gets up to give his sermon.

'I see from the people here,' he begins, 'that nearly everyone's first language is Hindi, so I will speak in Hindi this morning.'

Great.

'With the exception of John and his aunt,' he qualifies. 'And John is only the boss, so he doesn't count, and it will be good practice for him and he can translate for his aunt,' he adds mischievously. Everyone laughs – John rather ruefully.

'I don't know if my Hindi's up to that!' he mutters. 'I'll try and give you the gist of it.'

'Don't worry.' It's quite restful, actually, to have this respite. It's hot, despite the ceiling fans, and the sunlight outside is bright. The pastor has lost his shyness and come to life. He smiles and waves his hands and walks up and down as he talks. Every now and again he repeats a bit in English. John fills in with summaries of the rest and Nirmala, sitting next to me, helps out. Then they go silent.

You could hear a pin drop in here, if it wasn't for the whirr of the ceiling fans. I'm sitting thinking my own thoughts, when quite suddenly the Holy Spirit comes over me. I'm aware this is Christian jargon but I don't know any other way to describe the experience. It's an overwhelming, unmistakable sense of God's presence, combined with a feeling of being blanketed with peace. I wonder vaguely what Thomas is talking about but, to be honest, I don't much care. I feel held by God. Here, in this unfamiliar country surrounded by people I don't know, listening to a language I don't understand, I feel a sense of total assurance that God knows where I am and is right here.

Suddenly I hear a word I recognise. *Chapatti*. Indian flat bread. I wonder why he's talking about that? It seems to be getting a reaction from the congregation: they're shifting about and looking at each other. It is not boredom. Amazement?

John resumes translation duties. 'He prayed with a man last week who was dying of cancer. The family were all round him. When Thomas prayed, the tumour went down and the man sat up and ate, when he hadn't eaten for weeks. But also the Holy Spirit came down on the whole family – nobody moved for two hours.'

'Wow!' is my reaction. And I felt it happen here while he was just talking about it?

'What do you think of that?' John whispers.

Healing is something I feel very strongly about in Christian church life. It should happen, it does happen, it doesn't happen often enough, and far too often it gets regarded with deep suspicion or avoided altogether.

But this bloke is obviously facing the risks of failure and censure and is seeing God move.

'Can I interview him?' I hiss back. I know he doesn't work for Oasis and I'm here to interview the staff but I don't want to miss this opportunity.

When the service ends, John asks Thomas and he says he will talk to me.

'Perhaps outside,' he suggests, 'in the shade.' He seems nervous suddenly. Halfway out of the door, he stops and says, 'I don't know if I can do this. I don't think my English is good enough.' His English seems fine to me, but perhaps it is nerve-racking to be interviewed. Or perhaps he's uncomfortable with the one-to-one situation.

'Would you like someone else to come too? To interpret?'

'No – maybe it will be all right.'

'We could see how it goes, and if not I can ask John to send someone out to help?'

'All right.' Perhaps it's not his English but mine, I think. English is the second official language here, but a Hindi-accented version, with some different expressions. My English might well sound too foreign to understand. But he understood me quite well at tea-break. So what's the problem? I suddenly have the conviction that it's not the accent, nor the fact that I'm some foreign woman about to corner him with nosy questions, but that the only way to communicate with this person is to pray before I speak and let God direct the conversation.

So once we're settled outside on the chairs, I abandon my explanation about being here to write about the work of Oasis – after all, he's not working for them – and pray silently about how to open the conversation.

'Don't see him as an interviewee,' comes to mind. 'Speak to him as a pastor.'

He is sitting waiting for the interview to start. It's quite a long time since I talked to a pastor and I wouldn't really expect to, except in a crisis. The pastors I know at home are overloaded. So now I have the opportunity suddenly, I have no idea what to say.

All that comes to mind is my unexplained unease about the growing trends of life-coaching, self-development and 'psycho-spiritual' guidance in the UK. So I start there.

'I've come from the UK,' I start (unnecessarily. I think he's worked that one out, as I'm John's aunt) 'where people's lives are very much easier financially.'

Pastor Thomas nods. I doubt he spends much time with the financially comfortable in the work he does.

'People have a lot of material things and are constantly replacing them with newer things,' I carry on. 'But underlying it is insecurity. The message that we are constantly given, through advertising, television programmes, the culture of idolising celebrities – everything – is: You're not good enough. If your kitchen isn't the latest design, and your car, your phone, then you're nothing. And at the same time, we know people are starving and they have nothing, and it haunts us. We know we don't do enough to help, to make a difference. So we're not good enough there too – not even good enough as human beings.'

'Ah.' He's sitting forward, listening intently. There's no sign of shyness now. 'And that makes it worse – the insecurity.'

'Yes. It's a vicious circle. But we're not only getting that "not good enough" message from society: it comes from the church too.'

He has gone still now. 'The church?'

'The Christian churches in England tend to be very pro-active. The ones that are moving and growing are into social issues. Members are expected to throw themselves into activities and projects. Prayer is for old people who can't do anything physical. In my experience, to pray and do nothing else except what God is telling you to do is considered lazy and selfish.'

'Not good enough,' he muses.

'Yes. And the church in the UK can be very rational too – cynical, almost. Some Christian churches, you could attend for years and not really get any sense that we believe in the supernatural, or that God is a supernatural being.'

'Is that right?'

'It seems that way to me. So if people who aren't churchgoers have any kind of supernatural experience – whether a good one or something frightening – the church is the last place they go.'

'Where do they go?'

'A lot of people go to gurus. Life coaches, psycho-spiritual guides, New Age retreats, pagan rituals. Anywhere except God, Jesus Christ, and the Christian churches. What people are looking for is quite genuine. People generally aren't looking for trouble, or spiritual excitement, even. Some are, but only a few, I think. Most people just want some escape from confusion and inner turmoil. We have everything, in our society, but we're not very good at happiness or peace. That's what most people are searching for, but the places they're looking in are misleading and even dangerous.'

'We have our different forms of guru here,' he comments.

'Yes, but there seems to be some expectation of the supernatural here, at least. If you believe in healing, in many of the Christian churches in the UK, you're considered either naïve or weird.'

His eyebrows are raised. 'Really?'

'Most Christians I know, if they get ill, don't go to God to ask what the problem is as he sees it – not as a first resort. They go to the doctor first and ask the church to pray that the doctor will find the right diagnosis and the right remedy and that God will heal them that way.'

'Mm. No, we don't do that here,' Thomas says.

'Maybe it's because we have too much choice,' I suggest. 'If the doctor doesn't help, people can get a second opinion or go to a specialist, or pay to get treatment. But you were talking, in there, about miracles of healing as though they were an everyday event.'

'Actually,' he admits, 'in the last two weeks we have had quite a few.'

'We do have miracles in our churches,' I allow. 'They do occur: I've seen quite a lot over time. But they're few and far between.'

He furrows his brow in bewilderment. 'But then how,' he says, 'do you get new people in your churches? Because we started with one small prayer group and now we are five churches, and most of the new people . . . no, actually, all of the new people have come because the Lord healed them or somebody in their family.'

There's a silence while all this sinks in. Then, naturally and unsolicited, he begins the interview. 'I understand what you are saying,' he says. 'Because I was not good enough for the work I do.'

I pick up the notebook and pen as he starts to tell his story.

'I was a sailor in the Indian Navy from the age of seventeen,' Thomas begins, 'and an alcoholic – a drunken sailor. When I was seven years married, my wife and I had no child. We had treatment but it failed. Someone in my ship told me to go to a prayer meeting, so we went and they prayed for us. It was an English meeting we went to and I didn't understand more than ten percent of the words; my language is Malayalam, from the southernmost part of India, Kerala. But even though I didn't understand the speaking and teaching, still the spirit of the Lord touched me.'

This struck me as similar to the experience I had in the church while he was preaching in Hindi.

'I totally changed: I quit my drinking and we stopped the treatment, believing that if God is in it he will give a child. Six months later my wife conceived; our son is sixteen years old now.

'In 1994 I left the Navy. I was in Bombay and going to go back to Kerala but I asked a boy to pray and his answer from the Lord was a verse from the Bible: "If you stay in this land I will build you up." So I stayed in Bombay, but I got a very bad job – as a security guard – long hours, no time for the family, no time to go to church. I was tempted to think I had got it wrong – Satan told me it was not the Lord who had told me to stay – and two more opportunities came up to go to Kerala, but I didn't go.

'I hadn't done anything in the church; my English was not good and I couldn't speak or preach, and I couldn't sing – it disturbed and offended people! All I did in church was pray, or give a short testimony, telling people I had been a drunkard and the Lord changed me. This much was within me; I had a zeal for the Lord. But one day I felt the church I was in was not growing. And I felt for the people who sat at the back of the church, feeling like me – that I couldn't do anything. So I prayed for them.

'I met a boy on the road and it became a friendship, but one day he was not there and someone told me where he was living and I found him very sick. I thought of taking him to the hospital but I just prayed, and immediately he got healed. I said, "He will eat and drink today and in two days he will be on the road." I felt the Lord showing me this and I said it in faith, and it happened.

'I went to the same family and prayed for the mother and others, who also were not well, then I suggested we have a prayer meeting. I told my pastor, who only spoke English, not Hindi like the family, and he told me to start the meeting myself – but I am not the kind of person to start a meeting. I knew in my heart it was not an easy job. I didn't know the Word of God – my understanding of the Bible was not enough. I wanted to go and have some training but I was working seven days and hardly had even a half-day off so I had no time. But when I started a small meeting it was very powerful. God graced me and people started coming and the church started growing, and now we have five churches.

'We wanted to do many things in the social area. My cousin took a job with Oasis, and she invited us to their monthly prayer meeting. My wife has now joined Oasis as well. I went to the meeting and I felt God wanted a church-type meeting for the prostitutes at the drop-in centre, Aruna. I spoke to my senior pastor and to the Aruna team leader Sucheta, who told me she had been praying for someone to come and lead services. This time I thought God wanted me. We do our own church on Sunday morning and then we go there. We met with the ladies – ten or fifteen came. They experienced heal-ing and wanted to come out of the trade. We gave the prayer and waited. One lady was sitting singing and I felt the Lord wanted to touch her specially but the next meeting, she didn't come.

'The next week I prayed, "Let her come to this meet-ing," and she did come. She was having trouble with her eyes: they were always burning and she had spent a lot of money on treatment, but last week she came and said they were healed. Many of the prostitutes think what they are doing is wrong but their background is holding them: they owe money to their managers. One lady who has been rescued, I introduced to a man in my congre-gation, an ex-street person and alcoholic, and they are getting married. I felt God was joining them together. Tomorrow is the wedding.

'Before, I was preaching but I was not going to the people at the lowest level; I was just preaching. But going to the prostitutes and street people is Christian life; without this there is nothing. When we hear their stories our heart is touched – hearing the way they are sold out. It melts our hearts and encourages us to do more such work for the Lord. If you have a zeal for the Lord, anything is all right: your age, education, your job, even the things you can't do. Now when I sing, he uses it for anointing. And God brings the right kind of people, who are good in areas I can't do.

'I don't look back to the time when my job was rudimentary and I felt I had done the wrong thing. But I never forget what God has done; I never forget I was an alcoholic and led a bad life. I was nowhere. God's mercy! I am so satisfied. I feel at peace and joy in my ministry. God will take all the worry. So many times I have reason to get disappointed but at that same time God will show me a miracle. He keeps filling me, as things pull me down. We are seeing many miracles in our church. We have seen a lot in the last two weeks. Mighty things happen.'

I interrupt him here. 'What about when they don't? When you pray and there's no result? Does that happen with you?'

'Yes. Then we keep on praying. It's God's timing.'

'I've seen people healed of some quite drastic illnesses,' I tell him, 'but what's on my heart at the moment is people with AIDS, and children with autism. Even with all our medical resources, we don't have a cure for those. Have you seen anyone healed of them?'

'AIDS, yes. Well, we had a child with HIV who had very low immunity, a cell count of only three hundred. After prayer, the cell count went up to sixteen hundred. Now she is healthy and part of the church. What is the other condition?'

'Autism. When a child is completely withdrawn, has an aversion to human contact, doesn't communicate.'

'I don't know if it's the same thing, but one child who came to the meeting was abnormal, dribbling, made noises but had no speech. But after prayer he spoke the name of Jesus and then he went on to say other things, sentences that made complete sense. Last week I saw the mother and she says he can remember and write ABCD now.

'One man had two months to live – cancer. He couldn't even drink water, couldn't sit up. After prayer he ate three chapattis and is now going around the city. A boy had a swollen leg like an elephant's and his stomach was distended. A lady prayed and the swelling started going down.'

I think about my swollen legs, which are starting to get a bit painful, but it doesn't seem right to ask him to pray for me at this moment. I want him to go on talking.

'Why does God work like this in some places and not others?' I ask him. 'What do we have to do for Christ to come in this kind of power?'

'You must be ready,' he says. 'Revival is always there but the church isn't ready; the door isn't open. You must pray – unite in prayer with one heart. Whether a church has good singing or worship is not what counts, but quality of prayer and oneness of heart. If people are pulling each other down, even in a small way, Christ can't come in. If the leader is on fire for God, people will be open. I pray with only a few others – four or five, not everyone – and we are open and honest with each other, accountable. Then we see God moving. God will provide.'

The sound of singing is coming from the church. The meeting finished, the staff of Oasis are praying again. We get up and go and join in.

Chapter 6

Seeking a Ray of Sunlight

Two members of staff, a young man called Sachin and a young woman, Manju, are going to take me back with them to the project they work on with three others – Aruna, the drop-in centre in the red-light district. Aruna means *Bright Morning Sun*.

It's a beacon of hope for women trapped in prostitution, a place to drop in and chat, to receive encouragement to go for health checks and to find safe care for their children, out of school hours.

It's also, for many, the first step towards escaping the trade – the next step being the Oasis halfway house, a safe place to live, with the opportunity to receive counselling and health care. From there, some go for vocational training at the Oasis training centre I visited yesterday, or are helped to go back to their family or into hostels. Thirty-five to forty have been rescued, Sachin and Manju tell me on the way to the station, including Tiya who is now one of the Aruna staff working with them, and Shoba, the girl Pastor Thomas mentioned, who left the trade and is getting married tomorrow.

A train comes and Manju pushes me gently into a carriage. It is very crowded so I'm quite glad to be nannied. We sit down: the two of us.

'Have we lost Sachin?'

'Further down the train,' Manju says. 'This is a carriage for ladies only. Ladies can go in the men's carriages but men can't go in the ladies' ones.'

I hadn't noticed but, looking around, all the other passengers are women.

A woman standing up with a tray of hair ornaments waves her hand in my face.

'People go up and down the train selling things,' Manju explains.

The waving hand becomes a bit aggressive. I watch the other women's reactions – they avoid eye contact with the seller – and do the same. John tells me later about the fish-sellers: women who travel on the train carrying trays of fish on their heads, shouting out to people to beware of the stinking fish water. If it gets on your clothes, he says, people avoid you all day. Everyone gives the fish women a wide berth. They are guaranteed a space on even the most crowded trains.

Getting off the train, Manju keeps a tight hold of my arm and pilots me safely through the crowds. I can't see how Sachin will find us again but he does. They tell me about the other three members of staff – Tiya, who has a day off today but would have been great to interview, they say regretfully, because she started off 'in the trade' and now promotes health awareness among the girls and helps the children to study. Lizzie, Pastor Thomas' wife, is also not in today because she is not well; and Sachin's colleague Moses has gone to visit one of the men in hospital.

'Sachin and Moses work with the pimps and the clients,' Manju explains.

'Do they listen to you?' I ask Sachin.

'We're starting to build up relationships with some of the pimps. The clients are more difficult; they just want to disappear, but we are meeting a regular customer now. Many men have HIV and we help them with concern for their health. TB and addiction problems are common as well. We are counselling three men who are in rehab at the moment.'

'And we go into the brothels now as social workers, trying to help,' Manju says, 'and build relationships with the madams as well. Some of them come into the centre.'

'How do you feel towards them – the pimps and the madams,' I ask, 'seeing how they're exploiting the girls?'

'We try to reach out to them all with the love of Christ,' Manju explains, and Sachin nods agreement. 'They all have their own history.'

'We try to talk to the customers and tell them what kind of life the girls have,' Sachin says, 'and if they are shocked, then we say, "But you are causing this." They haven't seen it that way.'

I'm surprised that any of the people profiting from this lucrative trade are willing to talk to Christian charity workers at all.

'We have 24-hour prayer once a month, with three or four churches joining in,' Manju says, 'and it's after those prayer times that we notice a breakthrough – things happen that we didn't expect. Two girls left the trade this month.'

'Where do the girls come from?'

'They are widows or have broken relationships or they are poor,' Manju says. 'Shoba came from Kerala to Mumbai with three or four others to get a housework job through an agency. Her brother and father were alcoholics and she couldn't go home. But the agent cheated them, took the money and sold all of them. Shoba was sold to a brothel keeper for 30,000 rupees, and she became HIV Positive.

'She only spoke Malayalam, so I talked to her in Malayalam and taught her culinary, beauty and embroidery skills and also gave her counselling and shared the word of God and worship. She was in debt because she'd bought some gold rings, so Oasis paid the debt. She got out of the trade and is getting married now.'

We turn down a series of narrow streets. Manju points out the main brothel in the area. Aruna is right opposite it. She and Sachin go up the steps and push the door open.

Like the training centre, the accommodation is simple but the atmosphere is relaxed. A woman with sad eyes is sitting on a low platform topped with cushions against the opposite wall, under the window which looks out on the brothel, so close you could almost reach out. The windows of the brothel look out on nothing; they are shuttered.

Manju introduces Haneefa: 'Our peer educator. She has been in the job a month. She used to be in the trade and now she helps the girls. And this is Rupa, one of our beneficiaries.'

I have a second's confusion with the word 'beneficiary', mixing it up with 'benefactor' before realising Manju means she is one of the users of the drop-in centre and is therefore 'in the trade'.

Rupa, in a long pink *shalwar kameez*, smiles and offers to make *chai* for us. We go through to the kitchen and meet Maya, the cook, who smiles shyly and says hello.

'Maya has her own history,' Manju says.

Between the reception room – which includes an office corner with a desk and two filing cabinets and a lot of wall-art bearing witness to the presence of children – and the kitchen, there is a room full of bunk beds, where a number of children are asleep.

'They've come from school,' Manju explains. 'Later they'll get up and do their study. Come and meet Jaya.'

Jaya, a slim young woman from the Salvation Army, explains in clear English that she tutors the children so they keep up at school and they're not discriminated against.

'Only the teachers at school need to know who they are,' she says. I'm not sure if this refers to knowing they are children of prostitutes or to the fact that some are HIV Positive, but I guess both. The children learn Hindi and Marathi and are trying to learn English. 'We are raising their expectations as well, teaching them, "You are special to God and must fulfil your purpose for God." Today they'll have special games and stories because Fridays are Good Friday here!'

She goes into the children's dormitory and I sit down with Manju and Haneefa. Sachin answers a phone call and tells us it's from Moses: the man he went to visit in hospital has died. He's on his way back to Aruna and wants Sachin to go with him to arrange the man's funeral.

Manju tells me about the halfway house for girls who want to leave the trade. 'If they show willingness. We have to be sure they mean it; we don't let them just come for a holiday. There are seven girls there at the moment.'

'And their children?'

'No. The children go to Purnata Bhavan[5] or other organisations take them. The women stay for nine months to a year at the halfway house and do tailoring or beautician courses and literacy training. Discipline of work is difficult for them at first. Every Sunday there's church, with each girl taking responsibility for leading worship, choosing the songs, and so on.'

'The girls must come from all different backgrounds,' I suggest. 'Do they resent being included in Christian worship?'

'No, they understand that we're Christians and prayer is essential to our work. Thomas started a church here four months ago and people come and send their children. They don't have to. But prayer shines a light into the brothel: it's like a spotlight going out from the tower.'

'I met Thomas,' I told her. 'He's doing some good stuff.'

She beams. 'He's my cousin. Listen, talk to Haneefa now. Sachin is going to phone out for some lunch for you, for later on. Here's the list; say what you want.'

She waves a take-away menu. I'm not hungry. My swollen legs are throbbing and I'm grateful for the custom of everybody taking their sandals off as they come in the door – the floor tiles are nice and cool underfoot.

Manju points at the menu. 'Vegetables and rice.'

'Fine. Thank you.'

I'm still unfamiliar with the money and have to read each banknote before I know what it is.

'You don't have to pay now. When the boy comes.'

But I hand it to her anyway. It's easier to work it out now. She gives it to Sachin, who makes the phone call. Being a foreigner is like being a child. It reminds me that children have little control over their lives. Especially the children of prostitutes, perhaps, like the ones asleep next door.

Haneefa, the peer educator, is ready to tell her story now, with Manju as the interpreter.

"I was more than ten years in the trade,' Haneefa starts. 'My husband left me for another woman and my friend's husband sold me into the trade for 20,000 rupees. I had no source of income, so I had no choice. I had to pay off my debt.'

'What debt?' I ask Manju, thinking of Shoba and the gold rings she had bought.

'All the girls have debts,' Manju explains. 'It's not really their debt but it's called that – it's to the madam of the brothel, paying off the money she paid for the girl. They have to work until it's paid. They get fifty-fifty of what they earn.'

They are sold – into slavery – and then told they owe the person who is exploiting them?

Manju sees the expression on my face. 'I know,' she says softly. She gestures to Haneefa to continue her story.

'I wanted to live for something good,' Haneefa says, 'but I saw no way out. I'm from Karnataka in southern India and in 1992 there were riots and I went back home but I got injured in the riots, as you can see.' She points to the scars on her face and arms. 'And my son died; he was nine years old. So I came back to Bombay.'

'Why did you come back, Haneefa?' I ask.

'I have no family,' she says. 'I stay in the brothel. I have no home. I felt it was forever; my hope was totally gone. Then I met one of the Oasis staff, Moses, and he invited me to come to Aruna.'

'What was it like, coming here for the first time?'

'The first time I was a little bit scared,' she admits.

'What scared you?'

'Hearing Jesus' name. I'm from a Muslim background and I didn't understand when they sat round and prayed. But I pray to Jesus now because I believe. I pray for the people who helped me and for the girls who come here.'

'And you help the girls now?'

'Yes, I encourage them and go with them to hospital for health care. I was very happy to be offered the job as peer educator. I like to work with the rest of the staff and live like them. Just trying to make money is not satisfying, but being paid money for a good job is value. I feel my life has value now.'

Moses has come in while Haneefa is talking and has stayed over by the desk, careful not to interrupt, but Manju waves him over.

He and Sachin need to go out, he says, to make funeral arrangements, but he will be back by the end of the day.

'John has asked me to make sure you get home safely,' he tells me. 'I live in the same direction. I can't come in the taxi with you because I have my motorbike but I'll ride along with the taxi and see he goes there.'

'That's really kind of you. Thank you.'

'Welcome.'

I was slightly anxious about giving directions to a taxi driver who may not speak much English, when I have no idea where I'm going. I've yet to see a street name or road sign or many directions to anywhere! So going home with an outrider is a great idea. Or so it seems at the time.

Shortly after Sachin and Moses leave, two young women come into the centre, leave their sandals by the door and settle cross-legged on the other low couch, at right angles to the one we're sitting on. They have brought exercise books with them which they open and they start copying the outlines of the Hindi alphabet. They are wary and give frequent sidelong glances as they sit there in silence.

One, with darker hair and complexion and a heavier build, has a brooding expression. She fidgets and shifts and seems uncomfortable with herself. The other, immaculately dressed, graceful in posture and with a really beautiful face, is reserved and still. Like Haneefa, her expression is of sadness. After a while, observing Haneefa, Manju and me chatting, the first girl addresses a remark to Manju, who answers them both.

'They're asking who you are,' Manju tells me. 'I'm telling them you're a friend of Oasis who is writing about our work and asking if they're willing to tell you about themselves.'

They don't look willing. Their expressions are just short of hostile. I can't blame them.

I decide to speak to them directly in English, rather than to Manju. She's doing really well with the interpreting, which is a demanding task.

'I'm hoping that what I write will be read by people in the UK and other countries,' I tell them. 'You don't have to talk to me or answer any questions you don't want to. But there are people there whose lives are much easier than yours. They may not understand what it's like. They may even judge you.'

Both nod vigorously at this, as Manju translates, and make eye contact for the first time.

'So if you'd like to talk to me, it's your chance to tell them about your life. I'd like people to read it and think, "But that could be me!"'

There's a silence after Manju relays this to them. The second girl ducks her head and writes in her book, careful copy-writing like a child at school.

The first girl puts her book down on her crossed legs and settles herself more firmly.

'I'll talk to you,' she says.

At this point, as she looks me in the eyes and prepares to face the questions, a sense of complete hopelessness overwhelms me. I don't know if it's coming from her – there did seem to be a heaviness or an oppression that came in with them – or whether it's my own feeling that I have no right to question them. How can I ask them how they feel about their lives?

Manju is waiting for me. 'Go ahead,' she says. 'You can ask what you like.'

I nod but can't speak. Grief stabs me like a physical wound in the heart. These girls are the age of my nieces who live free and competent lives with careers and friends and parties and relationships they have chosen freely – not sold into slavery and serially raped every night.

After a moment, Manju starts off on her own, asking the questions and relaying answers to me. The girl is called Esha; she and the other girl, Sharmila, work in the brothel opposite and they come into Aruna on weekday afternoons for literacy lessons. Esha came to Mumbai in 2001, Manju says. Esha here takes up the story.

'I'm from Assam. I married a man there and we were together for three years but then he died. I got a lot of pain from this marriage and I didn't want to take the risk again.

'A lady invited two of my friends and me to Mumbai for a week, sightseeing. The first evening in the hotel, the lady bought us all cold drinks but she had put drugs in them. My friend told me that a man came in the night and abused me, but I didn't know this at the time.'

Sharmila, sitting next to Esha, forgets to write. She doesn't look up from her book but I can feel sympathy flowing from her to her friend. She is listening intently to what Esha is saying, though she must have heard it before.

'Next day,' Esha continues, 'I got up and the lady and a man came to see me. I had to stand in front of them while they looked at me and discussed.'

My voice returns at this point. 'Were your friends there?'

'I was alone,' Esha says. 'They had already taken my friends. Then I was taken by some other people to a different place and the lady told me I would have to stay there. I couldn't understand their language; I spoke a different one.'

The same problem as Haneefa and Pranad, the railway platform boy. India has over three hundred regional languages and dialects. An Indian who doesn't speak Hindi, as many don't, is vulnerable in a city where their own language isn't understood – as much a foreigner as me, or more perhaps as English is the second official language.

'Forty thousand rupees[6] were paid by the madam to the man,' Esha continues, 'but it's counted as a debt that the girl has to pay. In the brothel the girl gets half what she earns and the madam gets the other half. It took me five months to pay off the debt. I couldn't understand what was happening and I didn't know where my friends were.

'Then I met one of the friends in the hospital and we exchanged addresses and she came to where I was. But then she ran away from the brothel and the madam told me I had to pay off her debts as well.'

'Do you see any way out of here?' I ask Esha.

She shrugs. 'I will stay here for another year and then go back to my home town. Sharmila is supporting her family back home so she has to stay.'

Manju leans forward and speaks earnestly to her. 'I'm telling her we can help her get out of the trade now,' she says. 'We can offer her a place to live, a beautician's course or tailoring course, education . . .'

Esha doesn't respond.

'How do you feel?' I ask her.

'I am very depressed.'

I want to ask the girls about their daily life but I don't want to be intrusive. I explain this to Manju and she relays it to them. Sharmila has stopped writing.

Esha answers without hesitation. 'I don't go to sleep till 4 am. I have to work all night, every night.'

'I have a friend who was in the trade for twenty years,' I tell her. 'She said the girls would sometimes refuse a client who seemed too unbalanced or dangerous. Do you have the right to refuse anyone?'

Manju translates this, and Sharmila speaks up for the first time.

'At the beginning I used to say no, but it was forced on me so now I don't say no.'

'We are used to it,' Esha adds.

That seems the saddest thing of all.

'I haven't had any peace in my mind since my husband died,' Esha says.

'When you're depressed, does it feel easier to let things go on as they are rather than change them?'

She doesn't like the question. 'I am not thinking about things too much,' she says, shrugging again. 'I'm just taking life as it comes. I drink and I sleep, and that's it; that's my life now.'

She picks up her writing book and stands up. 'Come,' she says to Sharmila, but Sharmila shakes her head.

When Esha has gone out, Sharmila says something to Manju, who translates, 'She says she would talk to you but her story is a long one.'

'Tell her I'm here for another week and I'm listening.'

Manju repeats this to Sharmila, who laughs and says, 'It's not that long!'

'I'm sorry,' says Manju, 'but I have to have lunch; I'm so hungry!'

I'm afraid if we ask Sharmila to wait, she will go. But interpreting is intensive and hearing the stories is distressing, and I wonder if some of the lassitude I felt when the girls first came in has settled on Manju too.

So we ask Sharmila to wait and Manju pulls out chairs at the desk and hands me the take-away meal while she eats a packed lunch from home. The food here is delicious, spicy and full of vegetables, but I'm too hot to eat and my legs are still swollen like balloons. I offer Sharmila a share of the food but she refuses.

Another girl comes in. She is wearing a long caftan and looks about the same age as Sharmila and Esha, in her twenties, but she couldn't be more different from the reserved, composed Sharmila. She rushes towards us and talks fast, waving her arms so her bangles jingle in time to the words.

Manju introduces her as Anjali and tells her I'm here to write about the work. Anjali speaks a little English.

'I'm tired,' she says. 'I like to talk but I must sleep now.'

'OK.'

'Tomorrow I'll talk to you, all right?'

'She's only here today,' Manju tells her.

'Maybe I come back later,' Anjali says.

After we've eaten, I go to sit down by Sharmila on the couch but Rupa shouts, 'No, no! No sit there!'

'Sorry,' I say. 'Is it your seat?'

'No.' She points at my balloon feet. 'Feet up,' she says firmly and leads me by the hand back to the office chair, pulling up another one as a footrest. Oh no. I don't want to sit here in state like a lady of the Raj.

'I'm just going to talk to Sharmila,' I tell Rupa.

'Talk here,' she says, and calls Sharmila over.

At least I suppose Sharmila will have more privacy, away from the others. Manju sits down and prepares to be the interpreter again.

'I have trouble understanding her accent sometimes,' Manju says quietly. 'She's from Calcutta and speaks the Bangla language.'

'Does she understand any English?'

'No, nothing.'

This could be a long interview.

Chapter 7

Mother and Child

Sharmila begins, 'I was married and I have a little girl who is six years old. My husband was in a terrorist group and planted bombs. He never listened to me. I begged him to stop, but he went on with it. He lost all the flesh from both legs in a bomb blast and was admitted to hospital, then moved to another hospital far away. The baby was very small so it was hard for me. I sold all the land and the animals I had, and my gold, and I got work in the farmhouse – very hard work – to get money, because my husband was ill.

'I had a friend who worked in Mumbai who promised me a good job. She said, "I will give you some housework and you can do a beautician's course." I said no, because of my baby, and the lady said, "You can come with your baby and work, with your baby." So I came to Mumbai with my baby and stayed the first night in a hotel and the second night in a building I thought was a hotel, but there was a lot of noise in the night and I couldn't work out what was going on and when I woke up in the morning, everyone was sleeping. Then I understood what kind of a place it was.'

She pauses here, which gives me a chance to catch up with my shorthand. I wonder how many of these stories Manju listens to in her day-to-day work. It is not a routine job, by any means. She's the same age as some of these girls, perhaps younger.

'I found I had been sold for 50,000 rupees,' Sharmila resumes. 'When evening came, the women were all getting ready and the men were coming to the door. And they told me to get ready and put on make-up and I said no; I wouldn't sit down with them. I was there fifteen days. I was not willing, so the madam told me to go to another house; she said I would live as family there and I would like that place better. The madam told the pimps to take me to this second place, but one of the girls told me the pimps were planning to sell me off for one *lakh* and said I would never get out then.'

A *lakh* is 100,000 rupees, a huge sum of money for a girl to pay off. The girl who tipped off Sharmila was probably right – it would take a lifetime to pay back if the pimps resold her for that amount. The money the girls are entitled to keep for themselves is held back from them until the 'debt' is paid, when they're free to leave the brothel – in theory. In the meantime they are given or loaned small amounts, but Manju says the girls tend to spend the money as soon as they have any.

'The madam had given me her number "in case there were any problems",' Sharmila continues, 'so I went out to phone her and say I was in a bad place. I thought she was trying to help me. But she didn't trust the pimps; that's why she gave me the number. She was angry with them because she had one plan and they had another – to make money for themselves and not her – so they got a beating. I didn't realise that they all knew each other and this second place was the same thing; it looked as though we lived as a family – but when the phone calls came, the women had to go.'

There's still no expression in her face or in her voice. She recounts the story of her second deception and sale as though it's beyond emotion.

'The manager used to drink and beat the girls, and took my child and put her in care. They said I could see her but they never allowed me to go downstairs out of the building. They said, "When you are clear of your debt, you can go out."'

Still no sign of emotion. She's very still, very controlled.

'During this time, my husband rang the police from the hospital and said this lady had taken me to Mumbai. The police found my baby in the hostel and asked where the mother was, and the manager said they didn't know the mother, but the police said, "How did the baby get here, then?" and threatened to arrest the manager, so he gave them the phone number. The police called the brothel and said my child was not well and I should come soon, so the madam told me just to go and see the child and come back, and sent the boy from the brothel with me, but when we arrived the police asked him to take them to the place where I had been staying and they arrested them.'

This is the first time I've heard of the police doing anything about this people-trafficking. It sounds encouraging.

'I stayed two days in the police station and had a medical check-up, then I went back to my home,' Sharmila says. 'The police back home wanted me to tell them everything, and the whole gang got caught and were given three months in jail.'

Three months doesn't sound a particularly heavy sentence for selling a woman to be raped every night and for taking her baby away.

'But they were wealthy people and they paid money and came out,' Sharmila says.

'They didn't even serve the three months?'

'No.'

'Bribes,' Manju explains.

Sharmila still shows no expression except resignation.

'My husband was willing to take me back,' she goes on, 'but my mother-in-law was asking questions about where I'd been, and there was gossip. I stayed one year but there was a lot of pain. My husband listened to his mother and started calling me names and then he divorced me. He still wasn't working, and there was no money to bring up my child, and everyone was saying bad things about me.

'So I left my child with my mother at home and just came back to Mumbai. I earned 70,000 rupees while I was in Mumbai but the boy from the brothel who had been in prison told me I had to repay the money. After six months I left but they didn't give me the full amount I'd earned, so that I'd have to come back for the rest of my money, and when I went home again I found my house was empty; everything had been taken.'

I can see why she said her story is a long one. Just when every bad thing that could happen has happened, it gets worse. And then worse.

There is still no emotion. The only sign of upheaval is that every now and again Sharmila carefully refolds the pleat of her *dupatta* scarf and settles it more neatly, with its ends flipped back over her shoulders.

'While I was in the brothel I fell in love with a boy who said he'd take me home to my native place and marry me, so I thought my life would change now. I got married and we went back and I gave my new husband the 50,000 rupees I had, but within three months he and his mother were giving me trouble. They didn't give me food or water and they told me they didn't want my child.'

And worse.

'So I went back to my mother's place. I was with my mother one year and my husband never called me or came back for me. I worked at making cigarettes but it was very little money. There wasn't enough for food and clothes and I had to take care of my child. So I told my mother, "I'll go out and make some money and come back," and my mother was crying.'

I feel God was probably crying as well.

'I came back to Mumbai and earned one more *lakh* and a good customer told me to put the money into a scheme and I took his advice. I got some land and also put some money in the bank for my daughter.

'My mother wanted to file against the second husband for divorce because he never came back.'

'Did you want a divorce?' I ask her.

'I told her to do what she thought best. She contacted his family and they said he had gone abroad, but he came back and called me, so I went back to him. Then he went abroad again and I didn't know if he would come back and keep me as a wife.'

It sounds as though she was leaving it to her mother to decide about the divorce, and her husband to decide if he wanted her. Perhaps she can't imagine being given the choice, or thinks that whatever she chose would be unattainable.

'What do you want?' I ask.

She doesn't seem sure what to answer.

I put the question another way. 'What would you like God to do for you? How shall I pray for you, when I leave here?'

'I am worried about my girl – if she grows up and knows about me,' Sharmila says. 'I have this land and I want to build a house but I have to make some more money. I could do some other work if I could get a good job, to keep us.'

It sounds impossible. She's only just learning to read and write, and where would she get a reference for this good job?

Manju lets out a sigh at this answer and sits back, exhausted. She must hear a lot of these pipe-dreams, and for the girls the dreams seem more attractive than the practical reality of the halfway house and training courses which could provide them with a way out.

'I'm sorry,' Manju says. 'I have to go. I have my baby at home.'

'I know. Could I ask her just one more thing before you go?'

'All right.'

'How do you feel about your life?' I ask Sharmila.

I haven't yet heard her say how she feels about anything.

The answer is swift and heartfelt – a different tone from the rest of her narrative.

'I don't like to do this dirty work!'

Something has changed here. It feels as though something has snapped.

'Can I just say . . .?' I ask Manju, but she's standing up and her face says she's had enough. She has taken a lot of the strain of this afternoon, emotionally and spiritually as well as the mental effort of interpreting. But I need to say this to Sharmila.

So I say it to her face, in English, even knowing she doesn't speak a word of it.

'You've done so much,' I tell her. 'You've tried so hard to put things right, over and over again. Do you think it's time just to receive now? To let people help you?'

Sharmila starts crying. She clenches her fists in an effort to stop.

She turns to Manju and gestures incomprehension. Manju, bless her, sits down again and translates the words. Sharmila is now crying even more. I go and fetch my bag and give her a packet of tissues. Manju takes one out and hands it to her.

'Would she be willing to let me pray with her?' I ask.

'I think so,' Manju says. 'I'll stay and pray too.'

'Only if she's OK with it.'

She asks and Sharmila says yes.

Haneefa and Rupa are sitting quietly at the end of the room. I call them over and ask them to help us pray. Manju sits and holds Sharmila's hands, while the other three of us stand.

I don't want to pray in silence: it means the only sound will be Sharmila sobbing and that would embarrass her. Praying aloud in English would mean Manju has to go on interpreting, and she's tired. So I pray in tongues, as a way of letting God's Spirit take over, using whatever words or sounds happen to come to mind. That way we're even: nobody understands a word except God, who after all is the only One who can do anything in this impossible situation.

I pray till Sharmila has stopped crying and gone very still. We sit down and wait for her to come back to herself. After a while she gets up and hugs me, then Manju, then without saying a word she goes out.

Across the street, back to the brothel. It's such a short step. And such a long journey to make in the opposite direction.

It is such a hard thing to say: 'Help me.' What happened to these girls when they had offers of help before? It is so hard for them to trust anyone.

It would be hard to leave the brothel, too, leaving behind the money they've earned, if the manager insists that their 'debt' is still unpaid. For some, like Haneefa, it's become their only home. For Sharmila, ostracised by the gossips at home, it's the only place where she can be sure of not being judged, because the other girls understand.

The saddest thing seems to be the girls' acceptance that their 'debt' is a reality. They've bought into the myth that they actually are not free to leave because they owe their captors a refund; that a life that never belonged to the slavers and which they have exploited mercilessly to make themselves money, must not cost the exploiters the loss of a single rupee.

I wonder if it's extra difficult for someone raised on the Hindu doctrine of *karma*, which means literally 'deeds': the necessity of paying off the debt of one's bad deeds by good deeds and by suffering, not just for the duration of a lifetime but for a succession of lifetimes.

In that context, can it make sense, the message these Christian people keep telling them – that the debt other people have dumped on them isn't binding, that any genuine debts (like Shoba's, for her gold jewellery) can be paid off for them, and that they can leave the past behind them and walk free? And that Jesus is all the payment any spiritual 'bad deed debt' needs?

What was it Manju said about the 24-hour monthly prayer vigils at Oasis? 'It's after we have these that doors open that we didn't think possible.'

Shoba got out. Tomorrow is her wedding day.

Will Sharmila, Esha and all the others manage to break the cords and go free?

God only knows.

The children in the next room have woken up and are standing sleepily in the doorway. Jaya is back and is preparing for their after-school tuition session. Manju has gone home and Moses has phoned to say he is on his way back to the centre.

Rupa is still around. She hasn't volunteered to be interviewed, seeming happier to assume the role of guardian angel, bringing me drinks and conversing in fragments of English. I ask her to direct me to the loo and she takes me by the arm and ushers me in the door.

As in other toilets here, there is a tap coming out of the wall, a bucket and a jug. I haven't quite worked out the purpose of all these and meant to ask Charmaine for instructions. There is no toilet paper and the cistern doesn't have any water in it and won't flush.

When I come out Moses has arrived and is talking to Rupa, and I forget to tell them before I leave that the toilet is not working and they need to call a plumber. Charmaine, later, tries hard not to laugh when I tell her this. 'There's never any water in the cistern,' she says. 'The tap in the wall is there to fill the bucket and you flush the toilet with that.'

'And the jug?'

'The jug is instead of toilet paper. You fill the jug from the tap and pour water over yourself.'

'But you'd end up soaking wet!'

She gives up on the attempt not to laugh, and says kindly, 'I'll give you a packet of tissues to carry with you.'

Some toilets have a hose coming out of the wall as well as a tap. Without the necessary expertise I don't even contemplate that.

In the centre the children, having summed me up from the doorway of the dormitory, decide it's safe to come out. Seeing my camera, they're keen to have their photos taken and shriek with laughter at seeing their images on the little screen afterwards. Rupa has her photo taken with Moses, while he's on the phone. He looks tired but is satisfied that the funeral arrangements for the man in hospital are in place.

We leave the children with Jaya, say goodbye to Rupa, and go down into the street. Moses sees the taxi waiting and speaks to the driver. No go.

'He won't take you,' Moses tells me.

'Why not?'

'I don't know. He doesn't want to go there.'

'Are there other taxis around here?'

'No, they don't come into this area. What I can do is go off on my bike and try to find a rickshaw, if you wait here.'

I'm not that keen on waiting here, actually. I'm past the age of being trafficked but you never know: someone somewhere might have a fetish for middle-aged white women with inflatable ankles.

'Or you could come on the back of my bike,' Moses says, 'but I don't have another crash helmet.'

On the other hand, I'm not that old, and I used to ride pillion when I was a teenager.

'OK,' I say.

'Only,' Moses says slowly, 'John told me, "Don't take my aunt on your bike, Moses, because my uncle will kill me!"'

He's probably right but I feel disinclined to let Moses out of my sight. And the name reassures me. Parting the Red Sea is probably the best training ever for riding a motorbike through Mumbai rush-hour traffic.

'Tell John it was my idea,' I suggest.

He grins. 'OK.'

I get on the bike and we move off, weaving out of the side street and into the main road traffic. And what traffic! There is hardly an inch between the vehicles. Moses turns round and shouts something over his shoulder that I can't catch.

'Sorry?'

He twists round further, without slowing down as the bike heads directly into a tiny space between trucks. I wish he wouldn't. Whatever he's saying, it's not worth the risk of hearing it.

'I am good driver; don't worry!'

'You must be,' I shout back, 'to have lived this long!'

'What?'

Oh no. He is turning round again. I repeat it but he can't catch my accent. I try doing what John does and say it with a Hindi accent but even to my ears it sounds Welsh. On the third attempt, Moses understands me and turns back to face the front. Then he turns round again to laugh.

The road is like an assault course: with stock-car racing cars. And cunning little challenges like the odd block of concrete in the middle of the road, or a four-inch drop in the road surface. I find it easier to close my eyes, then realise I'm so tired that I'm actually starting to doze. Before I drop off – literally – I decide to keep my eyes open. Moses looks relaxed, swerving in and out among other bikes, rickshaws, cars and . . . yes, goats.

I wonder if I'm overestimating the actual risk of the traffic, as a foreigner unfamiliar with it, but Charmaine tells me later that accidents are frequent and often fatal. A few months after my return home, the husband of an Oasis staff member is knocked down by a rickshaw and dies of his injuries. The risks are real and have to be faced daily by the people who live in this city.

'I'll go slightly a longer way to the office,' Moses says over his shoulder now. 'There will be taxis there.'

I don't feel enthusiastic about going a longer way in order to get a taxi. 'I'm OK on the bike,' I shout back.

'What?'

Oh no. He's turning round again, leaving the bike on auto-pilot. But he's understood.

'It's too far, on the bike,' he says. 'You'll be too tired. This is best.'

'OK.' If it takes John over two hours to get home from the office and the office is some distance away, Moses is right.

We survive as far as the office, where Moses pulls over to the side of the road, having spotted a taxi driver.

'He's asleep,' I point out.

'No problem.'

Moses shakes the man awake and shouts instructions at him. The man, dazed, nods his head in what seems to be agreement. Moses opens the back door and says, 'You get in. I've told him I'll ride along beside.'

How can anyone ride alongside anything in this traffic? I thank Moses for the ride and wave him goodbye, fully expecting never to see him again.

The taxi driver, half asleep, starts the engine, which stalls. He restarts it and pulls out into the traffic without indicating. Half a dozen horns shout at him but he hoots back and carries on into what would be the centre lane if there were any lanes. Then the engine stalls again. He swears and jumps out of the cab. Brakes squeal and horns hoot but no one actually bumps into the car. And nobody shouts abuse.

The driver's head disappears under the bonnet. He jumps back into the car, starts the engine and moves off.

This happens again five times. There's no sign of Moses.

Six. Seven. Eight.

The eighth time, the driver is getting seriously embarrassed. He's not even swearing now. The car won't start again. I review the options, if he tells me to get out. I can ask him – in English – to flag down another taxi. But English doesn't seem to be as commonly spoken here as I'd expected and everyone so far has had trouble with my accent.

I can wait by the side of the road and hope Moses realises something's wrong and comes back. Only, he can't come back on this road because it's one-way, and if he does manage to turn round somewhere and come back on the other carriageway, he'd never spot me across all the traffic and in all the roadside crowds.

I can phone John and worry him, though what he could do I'm not sure. And, checking, I find I haven't got his mobile number on me. Also, my phone doesn't work here.

So I pick the one option that's left, and pray. 'Lord, please let the car start. And please ask Moses to stop and wait further on.'

The car starts. The driver drives off, muttering. Further on, Moses is waiting by the roadside. He flags the driver down.

'This is no good,' Moses announces. 'Pay him now and get back on the bike.'

Good idea.

The bike journey is very long. I think I'm still a bit jet-lagged, and the day has been full of stories, sights, sounds and experiences. I'm really tired. How much further can it be?

'I'm taking you slightly out of the way here,' Moses shouts, 'so you can see another red light district. Look up there!'

I crane my neck cautiously, trying to concentrate on staying on the bike.

Moses doesn't think I'm looking in the right place. He waves an arm and the bike, simultaneously. We swoop at an interesting angle.

'You see?'

'Uh?'

'Those windows. Behind the bars. The girls.'

'Oh, yes.'

God, they look like they're in cages. *Oh God, get them out!*

But what if he's saying the same to us? *How can you leave your own sisters like this? Get them out, now!*

But how?

'And outside the shops, on the street,' Moses points out.

They're so young. So lifeless. Beautifully dressed, motionless, hopeless.

The bike suddenly halts.

'I must talk to this lady,' Moses says. 'We've seen her before.'

He stops beside a tired-looking thin woman with a little girl in school uniform, aged about seven. She looks old to have a child of such a young age. But maybe she isn't old, just worn out. The child goes on red alert as the bike stops beside them. Her eyes are tired as well but wary, hostile. She clings tightly to her mother's hand, looking protective.

Moses speaks to the woman in – Hindi? Marathi? I can't tell the difference. She listens and her eyes brighten. He scribbles a mobile number on a piece of paper and gives it to her and she nods, thanking him, and goes into a shop doorway, holding the paper like treasure in her hand.

'I've told her, ring me; we can help her,' Moses tells me. The woman nods and tries to smile as he rides off. The child, unconvinced, stares after him.

We complete the tour of the district and head back on to the dual carriageway. After about an hour, I'm so tired I've lost my balance; it's an effort to hold on and I'm convinced I'm going to slide under the wheels of some vehicle and end up experiencing a Mumbai hospital. Or morgue. I also seem to have become an atheist. I can't imagine God keeping track of where I am. How could he, in all these crowds? I try to pray and can't remember how.

Quite suddenly, in the midst of the exhaust fumes all around and the fog inside my mind, I have a clear image of Pam, the friend and neighbour who introduced me to the church I attend. Her face is there in front of me, startlingly real, and I feel a sheer conviction that she is praying for me, if not at that precise moment then firmly enough to be banked in eternity and cashed in time of need. I need it now. And it helps. From being on the edge of panic, I feel a complete and unreasonable calm.

I recall, as a sixteen-year old with a boyfriend I loved dearly, pleading with my mother for the right to ride on the back of the motorbike he loved dearly, and winning only after she said, 'No! Not without a crash helmet!', a statement she regretted when his mother bought me a crash helmet. Now here I am, topping fifty years and don't-know-how-many miles per hour, riding on the back of a motorbike *without a crash helmet*! How's that for a long-delayed answer to prayer? So sit back and enjoy it, woman, and stop whinging!

Moses is turning round again. 'You are enjoying the ride,' he shouts.

Give a baby the name of an ancient prophet, and what do you expect him to grow up like? Insightful.

'You're right!' I concede.

'We can go a longer way round now and I will show you a slum,' he shouts.

On the other hand, Moses was also a man.

'Forget it!' I shout.

'Or you rather go straight home?'

'Home!'

He swivels round again to grin. 'I knew you were tired,' he says.

That's the trouble with prophets: always right.

Chapter 8

School Children and Street Children

The weekend goes quickly. Charmaine and I go to the girls' school concert on Saturday morning, while John takes Iain to the wedding of Shoba, the former prostitute.

Charmaine has warned me that Indian entertainments tend to be long. Eight hundred of the school's one thousand pupils are in the concert, which consists of a series of Indian dances, with formal, impassive movements and beautiful costumes in vibrant pink and orange, followed by three full-length plays. The girls are in *The Wizard of Oz*.

It's difficult for Christian parents sending children to the local schools, many of which are officially secular, like this one, but in practice are predominantly Hindu in influence. Both girls learn dancing as part of the main syllabus, but the dances are designed as acts of worship of Hindu gods and goddesses. Charmaine tells the children that these are stories, that dancing them is like acting in a play and doesn't represent their beliefs.

They are also taught meditation at school, but have worked out their own approach to this. When the other children are chanting the *mantras* – the names of gods – they say the name of Jesus.

After the concert we take a rickshaw to the shopping centre for lunch and to buy a *shalwar kameez* for me to wear when I go into the slum on Monday. The people who live there are not so accustomed to westerners. I'm amazed by the volume of material in the trousers; it feels like wearing a parachute. It will make sense when I join the women sitting cross-legged on the floor.

'How was the wedding?' Charmaine asks, when John returns.

'Everyone found it quite moving,' John says. 'The bridegroom in his speech said, "God's mercy kept her for me." When you think of everything Shoba's been through, and him too, that's quite an amazing thing to say – "He kept her for me."

'Shoba is HIV Positive, from her time in the trade,' he explains to me. 'We were afraid her husband was being naïve; we didn't know if he understood the risks. So one of us at Oasis had a quiet word with him when they got engaged, and he said, "But she's giving her life to me, so of course I would give mine for her."' He's silent for a minute and then says, 'It's what we're all about really – what we're here for. It was as good as it gets today.'

I must admit my reaction to the unimagined scale of need and poverty, driving through the city, was, 'How does a charity even make a start on this? Knowing that, however hard they work, they won't even make a small dent in the problem?' But now I've begun meeting and hearing about people whose lives have been touched by this work, I can see that – for the people who do receive – it makes more than a small dent; it makes all the difference in the world to their lives.

I have no right to be proud of this nephew, having had absolutely nothing to do with his upbringing or been closely involved in his life. But I do feel proud of him, and of his wife, meeting the needs of their family while making it a priority to regard all the unwanted children as their responsibility as well. It surely is one of the perks of being an aunt to feel proud of your nieces and nephews, and I'm happy to claim it now.

After putting the children to bed, John and Charmaine sit and we chat for a while. I ask about the girls from the brothel next to Aruna – how is it that so many have got trapped into prostitution in the same way: by some 'kind lady' befriending a poor family and offering to find the girl a good job in Mumbai? As the girls who reported this come from all different areas of India, is this a widespread scam?

'We know that traffickers work in gangs,' John says, 'and it's big business. But we don't know where the first point of contact is. This is obviously one way that girls are trapped.'

'Is there some way that families could be alerted that this is a trap and warned to refuse if some stranger offers to find a job for the girls? Local newspapers, perhaps?'

'People in the villages don't read,' Charmaine points out. 'What you need is to put something on television, because there is usually a television somewhere in the area. Or cinema would be better: a short film to run before the main film. When they put up a screen and show a film, *everyone* goes.'

'What would be ideal,' says John, 'is to get some Bollywood star to get the message across, then everyone would listen.'

On Sunday morning, church is held in a small cinema, reached by a narrow flight of cement steps from the city street. I'm not an urban person; I find it hard to live in cities where the horizon is always blocked by buildings. But there's something about real worship that takes you out of your surroundings and gives a sense of space, and for me that's the case here, among the small crowd of enthusiastic worshippers.

A man in glasses speaks about using every talent and opportunity for God's kingdom. I wonder again about life coaching: isn't that about encouraging people to use their talents? And aren't Manju and Saby and Smita and the others doing the same thing – spending their time encouraging people to learn new things and change their lives, for their own advancement and quality of life? And isn't it all 'for God's kingdom' – isn't that what he wants for us, the 'fullness of life' Jesus spoke about?

I don't know. I still don't know and I'm not going to try to work it out. Something doesn't feel right about this 'lifestyle' industry. How can you separate 'my life' from 'life'? I don't think, even though we're sitting here listening to Jesus' parable about using the talents we're entrusted with, that Jesus meant my life to be divided into segments and rated on performance, nor that 'fullness of life' is about setting goals and exceeding targets. That's management theory; it doesn't apply to life, unless life is an office.

During the last song, I feel overwhelmed by sleepiness and heaviness. My legs have suddenly swollen again and are throbbing, so I sit down. The service ends with everyone praying in little groups with the people around them, then chatting over *chai* and coffee.

At home Charmaine, who helps with Sunday school, shows me the set of posters the pastor has given her. In glorious technicolour they show Adam and Eve, Abraham, Moses, Noah, Elijah and others. Eve has flowing blonde hair and Adam is a white-skinned Tarzan.

'All white,' Charmaine comments. 'I don't really want to teach these stereotypes to the kids.'

'Who produced the posters?'

She looks at the back. 'Some Bible organisation.'

'I'd write to them and complain. It's really inappropriate.'

'And inaccurate,' Charmaine points out. 'In the Bible, they all came from Africa or the Middle East. These remind me of the pictures in a book my parents had in the 1950s – when everyone important was white.'

John is outraged. 'Tell the minister you're not using them.'

'I don't like to complain,' Charmaine says.

'He should complain, and send them back to who-ever sent them!'

The afternoon gives me a chance to play with the children and get to know them a bit. We try out face painting, read, play Bob the Builder and, inevitably, watch *Balamory* on video.

In the evening John, Charmaine and I pray together briefly for the week ahead.

John remembered to phone Archana, so for me Monday morning will mean a visit to Ashadeep – the centre for children living on the street.

*   *   *   *

I've got used to the sound of the ceiling fan. The first morning, I woke up thinking there was a storm going on outside. I know now that there is no storm and the weather outside will be as it is every morning – some-times hot and hazy with smog; sometimes hot and clear; always hot.

This morning, Monday, I drive into town with John to meet Archana, who will take me on a walk round Kurla station where many of the street children hang out now.

On the way there, in a traffic jam, I notice ladies in saris going round knocking on car windows, selling garlands and charms for good luck or for offering to Hindu deities.

'They're eunuchs,' John says, when one comes to the window just as the car moves on.

'They're men?'

'Yes, castrated men. It's a cult, a very closed community. They take boys at about the age of twelve. People are very afraid of them. They take money in return for giving "blessings" – the downside of it being that if they're not given money, they curse the person. People invite them to weddings.'

'Invite them to weddings? If they're afraid of them?'

'To bring luck and avoid being cursed. One came over to Charmaine when the children were in the car and offered to bless the family, and she said, "We don't need your blessings; we're Christian." So the eunuch cursed her and the children. Charmaine was so enraged she got out of the car and chased after him – and said, "How dare you curse my family? We're protected by Jesus Christ. Take your curse back and have it yourself!"'

'What happened?'

'The eunuch came back to the car and said sorry. They never do that!'

'Good for Charmaine.'

'She was always scared of them as a child. There's some kind of occult connection; no one's quite sure what they're into, but it's not good. They're very resistant to approaches by outsiders; they keep to themselves. There's some evidence recently that they may be involved in human trafficking.'

Charmaine tells me later that she was approached on another occasion. She and a European friend were at a crossing point, where the rickshaw zone begins, and a group of eunuchs homed in on them – 'probably because my friend was white and they were expecting money.'

As the group approached them, ready to offer 'blessings', Charmaine spoke first and said, 'I will bless you – in the name of Jesus Christ,' and they moved away. 'But one came back,' she said, 'and stood in front of me, very close, and said, "Did you say Jesus Christ?" When I said yes, he leaned right into my face and whispered, "Pray for me; I'm not well!" So my friend and I laid hands on him and prayed, right there in the street.'

Further along the road, in another traffic jam, John comments, 'There are a lot of different communities in Bombay with separate ways of life – like the tribal communities who live in the hills and don't really come into the city. And in the slums, there are different communities, all speaking different languages. Some come from Bombay and only speak Marathi, and others come from different parts of India. There's a gypsy community in Bandra slum as well.'

'Pranad, at the training centre, and some of the girls from the brothel said they'd arrived in Bombay unable to speak to anybody,' I recall. 'I thought everybody would speak Hindi?'

'No. In rural areas especially, people don't learn it unless they go to school.'

Archana is standing waiting for me and as John drives away she says, 'We'll walk around the stations and you can see for yourself how the children live.'

We walk through paved streets. In sunshine, everything looks better aesthetically but it doesn't help those living on the streets. The heat increases the risk of infection and disease. Food doesn't keep well and water and milk carry parasites. The crowds, as we enter the station, are wedged as tightly as in a football stadium. Preparing to go up a flight of steps and enter a covered walkway, Archana takes her knapsack off her back and straps it across her front. 'Be careful here,' she warns me. 'Mens are not good in this place.'

People are moving in both directions, forcing their way ahead. Men and women carrying large loads on their heads – piles of clean sheets, crates of fruit – barge their way through the crowd. I notice the fish-sellers John mentioned as well. I see what Archana means as I follow her, pushing our way through the crowd. The men walking in the opposite direction take advantage of the crush and the slow progress to grope the women. Even those further away flail their arms and stretch to grab any part of the anatomy of any woman walking the other way.

When we emerge, Archana takes me by the arm and says, 'We won't go across this bridge; it's too crowded. We'll go over the tracks.' She pauses at the end of the platform where the surface drops away in a dry mud bank, and follows a line of people jumping off it. As I scramble down after her, she says calmly, 'One moment,' and holds me back by the elbow as a train rushes past, a few centimetres away.

'Now we can go,' she says, as the roar of the train and the rush of wind subside.

We pick our way over the train tracks and she takes a detour behind the platforms over rubble-strewn waste land.

'This is where some of the kids come to pick up rags,' she says. 'They make a living by rag-picking. They fill a sack and get forty rupees. Some collect plastic bottles instead.'

I notice shabbily dressed children with bare feet walking across the train tracks, stooping to pick up scraps.

'How long does it take to fill a sack?'

'Maybe a day.'

'Forty rupees a day? They live on that?'

'They get sick a lot, especially skin infections. When they come into the centre, we give them medical attention and good nutrition: egg and bananas. And they have baths and learn to brush their teeth and wash their clothes.'

Three boys come over, holding rubbish sacks and smiling at Archana. She stops and chats.

'I'm asking how their friend is,' she translates after a while. 'A boy got beaten up over the weekend. A gang attacked a group of them while they were asleep, and he has head injuries. He was beaten before too. He told me he doesn't feel it now; he doesn't feel anything. They get like that.'

'Do these kids here come to the home?'

'They come to the centre sometimes. I'm asking them if they'll come this afternoon and they say they will come. I don't think these ones would come to live in the home – not now. They're too used to the streets and the platforms. That's where they sleep – over there.'

Just under the edge of the platform. Right by the tracks.

Some more boys come over, followed by a man who, smiling widely and swaying as he walks, holds out his hand as if to shake hands with Archana. She frowns and holds up a hand in a swift 'No' and he turns away. In contrast, her smile for the children is welcoming. Again, she listens to their news, congratulates them on the amount of scraps of rag in their sacks, and invites them to come this afternoon.

On our way to the centre, Archana tells me a little about herself. She is 28 and married with a two-year old son, and is a university graduate in English literature, but her heart has led her into this work with street children.

'At first we just went to the station where the boys were and we gave them colouring sheets and told them stories. We sat on the ground, I and another lady, and all the mens stood around. They told us, "They won't change," but the children told them, "Go! You go and do your work and we'll do ours!"

'After two months we rented a small place. About ten children used to come. Then one boy who had a wooden leg stopped coming and we went looking for him and he said some boys robbed his leg in the night. So we felt we must have a night shelter to protect children so they could sleep secure. We needed more staff for that – nine altogether. We used to bath them, cook food, and have activities – Friday was movie night! Then we took on a couple to run a children's home, for six boys at first. We were in Thane for six years and we've been here in Kurla only since October. Thirty children come, aged five to thirteen. We're here now,' she says, turning down a side street.

We go into a building and she unlocks a door and leads the way into a room with cracked plaster walls, adorned with brightly coloured posters of animals and letters of the English and Hindi alphabets, and sheets of picture outlines coloured in by children, accompanied by Hindi lettering which has been carefully overwritten in black and red.

'The children like colouring,' Archana says. 'We were amazed that they bought crayons with their own money; they are so keen. And when we teach them to keep themselves clean, the boys like to buy their own comb.'

Success is not measurable in results but in the immeasurable value of showing children they are cared for and loved, regardless of how they turn out.

All weekend, the prostitutes have stayed in my mind, and their difficulty in accepting the help that's offered. The Oasis programme seems a solution to their problems – it is a solution, a good and effective one – but they are people in shock, like survivors of a car crash who can't simply be hauled out of the vehicle and set back on their feet. They stay where they are, at the scene of the

crash, unable to move away from it physically or emotionally, even if by staying in that place they risk further
injury. If the charity staff were motivated by successful
results, they'd give up. But they hang in there, knowing
the value of doing just that. And sometimes the results
are unexpected.

Das, a staff worker, comes in and he and Archana tell
me about one boy, Moheet, who lived on Thane station.

'Most of the children there were sniffing solvent.
Moheet came to the day centre one day and left early to
work and we told him, "Don't go; you're too high."At
five o'clock we heard he had fallen from the train. I went
to the hospital and he had a big head injury and both
legs fractured. He was in hospital for one year and had
twelve operations. We went every day, one of us in the
morning and one in the evening. After the operations, he
had one leg shorter than the other. When he came out of
hospital we found a home for him but he wouldn't stay.
Eventually we found him a place in a training centre for
people with disabilities. He's seventeen now. We learned
that the seed that's sown can still bear fruit: he's telling
children now, "Don't sniff solvent: see how I lost my
leg!" God is in this business.'

There are special treats and outings arranged for the
children, but they enjoy ordinary afternoons in the centre too.

'The boys loved the Cinderella story!' Archana says.
'We thought it was more for the girls, but the boys were
in a world of their own, imagining it.'

It's easy to see how the story of an unloved child
who becomes beloved by royalty might appeal to them.
The mother of one boy, Sunil, dropped him in a dustbin
when he was born. Someone picked him up, then when
he was thirteen turned him out and told him to fend for
himself on Mumbai's stations. Older children who

come to Oasis may be offered a place at the training centre.

'Pranad was solvent sniffing,' Das says, 'and I told him he has to stop before he can go to the training centre. He said, "Tell me I'm going and I'll stop!" I thought he couldn't do it, but as soon as he heard he had a place, he did stop.'

Younger children are taken into Oasis' homes where they live in small groups with house-parents, or are referred to other charities, and those with addictions go to a Catholic detox centre. Two children so far have been adopted, one an eight-year old girl living on the station with her father who was a drug addict.

'We told him that anyone could kidnap her and take her to the brothels,' Archana says, 'and he agreed to let us find a home for her.' Fewer girls live on the streets, but many are abducted and trapped, hidden away out of view and beyond help.

I ask Archana and Das if they regard their lives as stressful and they consider the question, but not for long.

'We get tired,' Archana says. 'The children fight, or take a long time in the bath. And if children don't come in, we go round the stations. We pray a lot, in Ashadeep, but sometimes we are too tired to pray.'

'And sometimes we don't get Saturdays or Sundays off, if a child is in trouble,' Das adds. 'But after work we know we haven't wasted the day. The staff don't come here for the money or the job. At the end of the day, we are satisfied.'

Chapter 9

Restoring the Lost

I'm sad to leave before the children start arriving but I have an appointment with a slum. Archana walks me to the meeting point with Sudesh, one of the men who runs the Oasis project in Gyaneshwar Nagar slum in Bandra district. On the way we pass an old lady picking over a rubbish pile, and a barefoot boy of about nine, whom Archana recognises. She stops for a chat and he proudly reveals the contents of his plastic sack – a few broken plastic bottles. He smiles for the camera, with blackened and broken teeth, and waves as he walks away.

The street surface is giving way to sand and rubble and the sides of the buildings are patched with rusting corrugated iron. The smell is quite strong. Archana warned me to go to the toilet before we left Ashadeep: 'There isn't one at the centre.'

I meet Sudesh by a rickshaw rank and say goodbye to Archana. The rickshaw driver has bought one of the garlands of yellow and orange marigolds sold every morning by the roadside and has strung it up in his cab as a tribute to the gods and a protection for his rickshaw. On the short journey to Bandra, Sudesh apologises for his English.

'It has to be better than my Hindi!' I tell him.

I tried to learn a few phrases before I came but I didn't retain much. The construction of the language has some interesting differences: the use of the same word for 'yesterday' and 'tomorrow', for instance. And the phrase for 'I can't speak English' is 'English is not coming to me.' I think again of the preoccupation in the West with counteracting stress and finding inner peace. Perhaps it makes more sense, rather than saying, 'I can't find peace' – which implies effort is needed to search for it – to say, 'Peace is not coming to me,' which implies being receptive. But certainly, now I am here, Hindi is not coming to me. English comes to Sudesh more freely.

I ask him about the slum community and he tells me Oasis has been involved since 2002. The people who live there have seen many changes, he says, but it's still a difficult place to live. Kuldeep will tell me more, he promises. Sudesh and Kuldeep run the project, with other staff and volunteers and increasing participation by some of the slum-dwellers themselves.

When we arrive I see Bandra is not all slum, by any means. The shacks are a stone's throw from sophisticated apartment buildings and international banks in a thriving commercial area. The former marshland site with its patchwork dwellings is now prime building land, sought after by developers who repeatedly request meetings with planning officials and reportedly offer substantial bribes.

I follow Sudesh from the road into a network of narrow passageways. Children stop and stare at me. Wearing the *shalwar kameez* and a *dupatta* borrowed from Charmaine doesn't stop me from feeling conspicuously white and foreign.

'Hello-oo! How are yoo-oo?' sings out one little boy and the others behind him giggle.

'I'm fi-ine,' I reply in the same singsong tone. 'How are yoo-oo?' They rush away, shrieking with laughter. Further on when I look back they are there again, following from a distance. When Sudesh stops in front of the Oasis centre, they all stop too, bunching up together like cartoon characters applying the brakes.

The centre is one metal-shuttered unit in a row of continuous terraces, facing a brick wall. Downstairs there is one room, cement-floored, with a table, chair and cupboard at the front, open to the alleyway, and a curtain shutting off the back half of the room. It's being used as a health clinic at the moment, Sudesh says. At other times it's the space for the *balwadi* (pre-school) children.

Unlike other buildings in the slum, it has an upstairs room which is also multi-functional, being used for computer training, tailoring classes and an office corner. 'Upstairs' actually has no stairs, just an almost vertical metal ladder with a handrail.

I have a thing about ladders. On the farm where I spent a sizeable chunk of my pre-teen and teenage years, I never managed to get up or down the hayloft ladder, which was an almost daily necessity, without freezing with terror halfway, to the accompaniment of either encouraging comments or jeers and threats to shake the ladder, depending on who was around when I forced myself to scale it.

I also have a fear of dogs, especially strays – which run around in packs everywhere here. Also I'm not keen on getting lost, crowds, heavy traffic, extreme temperatures, loud noise or the large shiny black cockroach I'll come toe-to-toe with in the shower this evening. Crossing train tracks, being groped by passing strangers and risking being mashed on the roads are not favourites either. God obviously has me on an aversion therapy exercise while I'm here. I hope he's remembering to tick off the items on the check-list as I go through them so they don't have to be repeated. I flick my floating *dupatta* over my shoulders out of the way, clutch my bag, camera and notepad, and follow Sudesh up the ladder.

Upstairs, three women in *shalwar kameez* are sitting on the floor cutting out garments from newspaper patterns, while a fourth, wearing a sari, is seated at one of four treadle-powered sewing machines mounted on small tables. Along with storage boxes, this area takes up about half the upstairs space. In the opposite corner, a young man whom Sudesh introduces as Saroj, the IT teacher, is setting up a lesson for two students seated at computer terminals. Kuldeep, at his desk in the remaining small area used as office space, stands up to greet us. His manner is more formal than Sudesh's and his English is impeccable.

Charity project leaders need an interesting mixture of qualities. Like John, Kuldeep seems to have a strong business sense, retaining facts and statistics and combining a broad overview with an attention to detail. He has files and charts and a three-year plan for Bandra project and has made notes for the interview. It's when he starts talking about making Oasis redundant here within a few years and handing over to the people of Bandra slum community themselves, that it becomes clear that he is more than a businessman driven by the desire to achieve a successful project.

Having arranged for *chai* to be provided, Kuldeep sits forward and delivers facts.

Bandra slum occupies less than one square mile and comprises 5,600 families – about 25,000 inhabitants. It is not one community but five separate communities, each with their own language, eating habits and culture. They are from the local province, Maharashtra; from UP in the north; Andhra Pradesh in the south; a gypsy community from Karnataka in the south and a Muslim community. Hindi is the language by which they communicate with each other.

'The area was allocated to the gypsies in 1990,' Kuldeep says, 'but then others moved in. Bandra was marshland until the 1990s. Oasis started the project here in 2002 when the only homes were plastic sheets.'

Bandra creek still runs through the slum, now confined in a narrow channel chipped out of the cement path between the shacks. 'Originally Oasis came for the gypsy community,' Kuldeep says, 'but they refused because we were Christians. Then one community leader listened. Now the gypsies come as well, for post- and ante-natal care, medical care and family planning. A lady doctor and a child specialist come twice a week. On the prevention side, we teach hygiene.

'It was so dirty here. There was standing water, no sanitation, malaria, and most of the children had skin infections and boils. All 150 lanes are cemented now, and people used rubble to raise their houses above the water level. And every third house now has a tap outside.'

This sounds good; it's only later that I realise that, as in the rest of Mumbai, the water supply is sporadic so water doesn't come out of the taps on demand. The main items of furniture I will see in Bandra homes are containers of stored water.

'It was our objective that the community would start micro-enterprises and manage its own affairs so it wasn't dependent on funding. We decided to start with the women, because they have time free between 12 and 4 pm, and set up self-help groups.

'The community was in debt to moneylenders, at thirty to forty percent interest rates: they'd be paying it back for a lifetime. Now the Women's Federation – groups of ten to fifteen women, organised by lanes – meets every Monday and saves small amounts of money, which they put in one common bank account. After six months the group takes out a loan at a low interest rate – seven to eight percent – and decides together how much to give each person.'

'What are the loans used for?'

'For work or for emergencies – sickness, or having to go home. But the saving scheme is just a tool, to empower people. We are aiming for 2,500 members in three years; we have identified twenty-five women leaders who will go through a training programme on economic, educational, environmental and vocational training and health and social issues, and we are training mentors. They will take over each of the activities we are doing, and we will shift out to another slum where people have nothing. We'll leave this area to the Women's Federation, overseen by the local church which is our partner in the project. Some of the government organisations have recently started giving loans but they don't empower communities.

'Poor people can become dependent on loans, which become a handicap for them. I've seen very few people use loans in a positive way; they go from emergency to emergency. But if people use their own small amount of money, they value it and see God bless it. Once a month we have meetings in which we share God's word with people, and with the children.'

Are Kuldeep and his colleagues afraid the Christian ethos of their work will be lost, when they hand over the project to the community?

He shakes his head emphatically. 'No. This project is not our baby. It's the community's. We are helping them nourish this baby. We trust the community and I think they now trust us. Real transformation comes from Jesus and when we hand over this project, if Hindus and Buddhists do the same work then we trust that the spirit of Jesus will come through it.'

The women have set five priorities. One is special tuition for children not doing well at school. The second is small businesses. Many women do beadwork and jewellery-making but complain that the middlemen take too much. Oasis will help with sourcing the materials and supporting the women in setting up their own businesses.

The third priority is to restart an immunisation programme. 'We've told the Federation leaders – you speak to the local politician and we'll back you,' Kuldeep says.

The fourth is children's toilets. 'There's such a long queue in the morning that the children can't wait; they have to squat and they are embarrassed. And the original toilets are old and not well maintained,' Kuldeep says. 'The new ones are maintained by the corporation but cost two rupees a time to use.'

'How many toilets are there?' I ask.

Sudesh intervenes here. 'Four toilet blocks,' he says. 'Three or four toilets in a block.' He waits for the shock to register.

'For 25,000 people?'

'Before last year, only two blocks,' he says.

'How can they expect people to live like that?'

'The government is planning to clear this city of slums,' says Kuldeep, 'and demolish the houses.'

All this work, I think, and at the end of it they may see the community they've cherished reduced to rubble.

'How do you feel about that?' I ask the two of them.

'I personally feel there are three things that God will restore, if we are his instruments,' Kuldeep says. 'Faith, hope and love. What is achieved here is not by our strength or power but by God's Spirit. We are part of God's plan, to restore what is lost.'

To restore what is lost. Even if the buildings so carefully developed are crushed and the community that has learned to stand up for itself is scattered, the unseen restorative work in people's hearts will last. I don't realise I'm sitting here silent till Kuldeep asks if I'd like to interview some of the staff.

'What I'd really like is to walk round the slum and meet some of the people, if they wouldn't feel I'm intruding. Would they?'

'Of course not. Chandrakala will take you.'

Chandrakala is halfway down the steps when he calls her. She does a swift turn on the ladder and runs up again.

'This is John's aunt,' Kuldeep tells her. 'Will you take her into some of the people's homes?'

'Of course. Come!'

She bounds down the ladder again, like a mountain goat, and I follow her, like a geriatric gazelle.

Chandrakala, at 24, is one of the two *balwadi* teachers for children aged between two-and-a-half and four.

'I'll take you round the slum and you can meet Priya and Madhu and some of the others,' she says. 'They live in the slum and also help with the work.'

I'm having trouble with my *dupatta*. It doesn't stay obediently suspended over the shoulders like everyone else's. Chandrakala takes it from me and deftly loops it round my neck. 'Like that,' she says.

'Thanks.'

We go out and into the alleys, where the heat bounces off the walls of facing rows of terraced dwellings, which are close enough to touch on either side. I follow Chandrakala: there isn't room for two people to walk side by side. The ground surface of the alley is cement or slabs of stone, broken where water pipes have been laid. Walking space is taken up by doorsteps, plastic barrels of water, pipes laid above the surface and the narrow water channel – the diversion of Bandra creek – which is dark brown and bubbling, buzzing with flies and mosquitoes. Further ahead, a small child is peeing into it.

Lines of clothes and bedding slung across every wall
add a splash of colour to the brick and cement homes,
with their corrugated tin roofs. Some homes have doors,
some have metal shutters like a lock-up; others have
sheets of plastic. Few have windows.

A little boy is asleep on a doorstep, his hand trailing
the ground. Chandrakala dodges swiftly from side to
side of the path, negotiating familiar obstacles and stopping to say hello to the women sitting on doorsteps. A
few regard me suspiciously but the children are less ret-
icent. I produce a few sheets of stickers of flowers and
hearts and let the girls point to which one they'd like.
They deliberate over them seriously and advise one
another. I hadn't managed to find any more macho ones
so I think the boys won't want them, but they do. The
mothers start to smile then and call their children from
the dark rooms behind them to choose a sticker, and the
children call their friends.

Two young teenage girls and a younger sister stand
shoulder to shoulder across the alley, posing for a photo.
They are beautiful and know it, in bright blue and red
chiffons, with bracelets and earrings and wide smiles.
Chandrakala teases them, and they hold the pose till the
camera clicks, then collapse against each other, giggling.

One little girl of about seven, barefoot like the others
and dressed in a stained top and skirt, balances her baby
brother on her hip and stares at me. I offer her a sticker
but she shakes her head. When she sees the camera,
though, she stands still and waits. I show her the image
on the little screen and she looks at it from a distance. I
show her the stickers again. 'Sure you don't want one?
Or your brother?'

She shakes her head: still no.

Further down the alleyway, word has gone round and
a bunch of children has gathered. Turning round, I see

the unsmiling little girl has followed, now minus the baby. Has she changed her mind? No, she shakes her head slowly again.

When all the children have chosen, we move on. At the next stop, halted by shouts from two little boys dragging others who don't yet have stickers, I see the girl has followed us again. The boys call her and point at the stickers. She shakes her head. They urge her, pointing to different ones.

'*Nahi*,' I tell them. 'She doesn't want one.'

The boys stop shouting at her and she smiles, for the first time. At the next corner, she is right behind me, and at the next. She smiles at me above the heads of the excited kids. I haven't given her anything. Or maybe I've given her a choice, the right to say no? I don't know.

'Here is Priya's house,' Chandrakala says. We are in front of a lock-up, a rusted metal shutter lifted open a few centimetres at the bottom. Chandrakala calls out and the shutter is hoisted up. Priya appears, a little startled to see such a crowd gathered outside her home. She could have walked out of the pages of *Vogue*. Her yellow sari shot with silver thread, perfectly groomed hair, long necklace and loop earrings and the neatly marked *bindi* on her forehead (the red dot signifying a Hindu married woman) bear witness to a level of self-respect that is remarkable in this place where it must be so hard to keep clean.

'Priya speaks some English,' Chandrakala tells me.

'A little,' Priya corrects. She raises the metal shutter a little higher and waves us in. 'My home is small,' she apologises.

'Not too much housework, then,' I say, and she laughs.

'No, that is good.'

The room is about half the size of a garage, with no windows for air or light. On a mat on the floor lie two babies and a tiny child, asleep. A young woman sits on a bench attached to the wall, watching them. She gets up when she sees us and gestures to me to sit down. I leave room for Chandrakala and Priya but they're sandwiched in by the crowd and stay standing outside.

There are two plastic chairs stacked on the other side of the doorway but otherwise no furniture apart from containers of stored water and a neatly stacked bank of cooking pots against the far wall. But there are pictures on the wall and the floor has chips of coloured tiles laid out in mosaic borders.

'This is Priya's daughter,' Chandrakala introduces the young woman. 'This baby is hers. Take a photo if you like.' She looks questioningly at Priya who says, 'Please,' and smiles, but moves to throw a cloth over the baby, who is wearing only a vest. He whimpers and rubs his eyes but doesn't wake.

I'm hesitant about taking a photo of such an intimate domestic scene but everyone is waiting expectantly, so I click the shutter and people shift forward to have a look at the image.

This slum, with its contrasts of colour and squalor and its poignant images of ragged children carrying even tinier children, is a Sunday supplement editor's dream. Sandwiched between adverts for world cruises and celebrity lifestyle features it would provide the statutory slice of compassion between thick wedges of consumerism – and deliver one more message of confusion in a society that constantly preaches contradictory values. But Bandra is not a photo feature, the slum is not picturesque for the people who live in it, and these lives are in reality sandwiched between thick wedges of commercial development edging closer on all sides, threatening to bulldoze the real and vibrant life of this community.

The people in Bandra slum are not the worst off, by any means – better than the people by the roadside, or the construction site families living under plastic sheets.

But there's still too little to live on and too much to die from here. There's malaria and TB, gastric and skin infections, HIV, poverty, alcoholism, a high rate of domestic and neighbourhood violence, child abuse, and the ever-present risk of abduction and human trafficking. I take out my notebook and start to write as, with Chandrakala translating, Priya talks in Hindi about her work as a volunteer.

'I have a very positive attitude towards the Women's Federation started by Oasis,' Priya begins, 'and, from the beginning, I didn't have the fears that some of the women had about taking help from Christians.'

At this point, two of the women outside speak at once and point at me.

Chandrakala interprets. 'They want to know what language it is you are writing.'

'English,' I tell them. 'But shorthand. This is one word.' I draw an outline, shorthand for the word *shorthand*, and they lean forward to watch.

'English,' one child tells another but he stares at the page and then at me, knowing this is not English and I haven't got it right.

Priya laughs and continues. 'Through Oasis I got help – I sent my son for tuition and I went to them for medicines – and now I help as well, with ante-natal and post-natal care. I visit the women at home, check their weight, take their medical history and write up details of their family background, number of children, any operations and so on, and I encourage them to go to the doctor if necessary. When I heard about the self-help groups for women, to help us save money, I thought, "Ten or twenty rupees doesn't make any difference; why bother to save that?" But now I can see it does make a difference if you save it up and then we can get group loans.

'There are two other results from the Women's Federation meetings: the health teaching made a difference to my way of thinking, and the women came closer together in a group. If anyone wants to take a loan, they have to share with the others why they need it, so they are sharing their problems, which never happened before – people used to keep their troubles to themselves. So the women are getting to know each other better.'

'What would you say are the stresses of living in this community? And has it changed?'

Priya pauses for thought, then says, 'Before, there was nothing to do. I used to do my work and then sit and talk to the neighbours; there was nothing more. But now we can send our children to *balwadi*[7] and there is the savings scheme and learning tailoring, and helping visit the pregnant women, and I don't spend my time sitting thinking, "What can I do?"'

If I'd had to guess at the sources of stress of living in slum conditions, I'd have said the lack of privacy and sanitation, the insecurity, risk of eviction and risk of disease. I wouldn't have thought of boredom, and maybe that's something we forget about poverty – the boredom of it and the lack of choices.

Certainly not everyone here is making use of the resources offered by Oasis; many people conform – at least outwardly – to the stereotype of the slum dweller, dirty, dishevelled, hopeless or hostile. Many struggle to cope not only with the conditions of their present life but with a difficult personal history that makes it impossible for them, just yet, to move out of despair and imagine a better future.

But for every person who rises above the stereotype and takes advantage of the opportunities, many more are encouraged. Priya, a woman who not only survives in this environment but can dress beautifully, care for her kids, decorate her house with flair and then work voluntarily to help the wider community, is not – I would guess – most people's stereotype of a gypsy slum-dweller.

It isn't in human nature simply to survive. To live a human life surely involves a need to be creative and to contribute to other people's lives.

Coming away from Priya's house, we meet Madhu, who runs a women's literacy group in her home. She is going from house to house to tell them it's time to come but she agrees to postpone the start of the class and talk to me, and sends us on ahead of her.

There are several women already in Madhu's house, sitting on the floor making hair ornaments – a form of home-working popular in the community. The floor is paved with unmatching tiles, ends of lines.

I'm reminded by Chandrakala's example to take off my sandals and leave them at the door, and the tiles are pleasantly cool but Madhu, following us in, takes out a mat and spreads it on the floor for the visitors and we sit on that. After greeting the other women, I ask Madhu, with Chandrakala translating, to tell me about her life.

'The life here is very difficult,' she says. 'As a girl child, 75 percent of your life is your parents' life. I grew up in a small town and I got married before I had my education. After marriage I came here.'

'What was your life like when you came here?' I ask.

'Don't ask!' she says and laughs, then elaborates. 'This area wasn't developed then, not like it is now. People used plastic sheets to shelter them; there was no light, no water, no sanitation. We had to walk for ten minutes to get water and carry it back here, every day. We were only allowed one pot of water a day and we

had to pay ten rupees for it. Now there are a lot of facilities and if there is a problem, there's a solution. I think
I should be able to get some good job for my family. I'm
teaching classes: I got training in teaching at the Oasis
centre.'

'What are the stresses of living in this community, and
how do you handle them, personally?'

'Some people here are good,' Madhu says, 'and some
try to cause trouble, but we have to welcome anyone
who welcomes us. It's simple.'

'Do you feel secure here?' I ask. She looks secure,
seated in her two-roomed house with its patterns of
green dots painted across the walls.

The women have taken out worksheets and are
preparing for their class with her, their teacher. A baby is
passed from one to another as they take turns minding
him, and a toddler lies asleep in his mother's lap; she
rests her worksheet on his stomach and follows the outlines of words with her finger.

But can they feel secure here, when the government
regards their carefully improved environment as the
next move in its slum-clearance scheme?

'These houses are being taken down by developers,'
Madhu says. 'So the fear is there in everyone's heart.
People don't bother to make their house more solid
because it may go tomorrow. Every week there are meetings between developers; the posh area is very close and
they want this land.'

'Will they re-house you if you're evicted?'

'The government will offer other homes in outer
Bombay but we want to stay in this area. Our children
attend schools here and people have jobs.'

'Do you think, as a community of 25,000 people, you
would have any influence in speaking up against the
development schemes and keeping your homes?'

Here another woman intervenes. 'I believe people in this area can bring change,' she says.

An older woman disagrees: 'No, because these people in power are corrupt and only think about themselves.'

I go back to Madhu. 'What do you think?'

'I think we can bring changes,' she says slowly, 'if we work together and speak up with one voice.'

I hope they can. There is a real sense of community here, with the women sitting together to learn. I imagine them transplanted to the tall narrow high-rises built so close together that they block the light from each other's windows, on the far outskirts of Mumbai. Too costly to journey into the city to work; with no incomes, the new homes becoming new slums, their inhabitants would be marginalised once again and back to square one. Stress is written on the women's faces, as they discuss the situation. This is a discussion they have had many times and will have again.

Madhu suddenly makes a comment to Chandrakala and nods towards me. Chandrakala says, 'She's worried about your feet; she says they are swollen.' I'm amazed again. First Sanam and Smita in the training centre, then Rupa in Aruna, the red-light drop-in centre, now Madhu in the slum. How do any of them have compassion to spare for a symptom which must rate zero on the scale of their own problems – in this case the threat of losing their homes?

An unsmiling little short-haired girl of about five, clad in a shiny turquoise and silver sleeveless *shalwar kameez*, has been either standing or sitting in the doorway throughout the whole visit, alternately watching us all and looking up and down the alley outside, like a little doorkeeper.

I assume that she lives here or her mother is one of the women in the class, but I am wrong: she is waiting for us.

**Vocational Training Centre – former street boys –
Chapter 3.**

Pranad, former street boy – Chapter 4.

Haneefa and Anjali, Aruna drop-in centre – Chapter 6.

Children at Aruna centre – Chapter 7.

Rubbish picker boy – Chapter 9.

Rubbish picker woman – Chapter 9.

Slum family – Chapter 9.

Slum girl with brother – Chapter 9.

Slum: Priya – Chapter 9.

Priya's children – Chapter 9.

Slum girls – Chapter 10.

Slum: Nadira (right) with mother and sister –
Chapter 10.

Outside the slum – Chapter 10.

Purnata Bhavan children – Chapter 12.

More Purnata Bhavan children – Chapter 12.

Arun and John, Purnata Bhavan – Chapter 12.

Aari workers, Purnata Bhavan – Chapter 12.

Arun and Esther, Purnata Bhavan – Chapter 13.

Clare and Madhukshi, Purnata Bhavan – Chapter 14.

Bangalore – Chapter 15.

Roshni (right), and trainees – Bangalore.

Aditi, Bangalore – Chapter 16.

Waterfront, Mumbai – Chapter 17.

Clare, waterfront, Mumbai – Chapter 17.

Dhobi (Washermen's), Ghats, Mumbai.

Chapter 10

Meeting the Doorkeepers

'Come,' Chandrakala says, 'we'll go back to the centre now.'

But the little girl who has been occupying the doorway of Madhu's house has other ideas. She runs after us, shouting.

I turn and wave at her and say, 'Bye!' and she erupts with rage, running past me, jumping neatly over the water channel and standing in front of Chandrakala, puffing herself up to twice her size in an effort to block our path. She is making enough noise to compensate for her earlier patient silence and her diminutive height.

'What is she saying?' I ask Chandrakala.

'She's saying, "Come to *my* house now!"'

The child keeps on shouting and Chandrakala laughs. 'Now she's saying, "I make you *chai*, I give you cold drink, whatever you like – come to *my* house!"'

A cold drink sounds like a great idea. Except that I've been warned not to drink water or anything made from it in the slum.

'I think we'll have to go there,' Chandrakala decides, when the child refuses to let her pass. 'But we'll only stay two minutes; we won't sit down or drink anything.'

She gives this reply to the little girl, who breaks into a smile and rushes past us again, only turning back to make sure we're following as she dodges the broken stones and the water barrels on her familiar route.

Chandrakala follows her into her home, where a startled woman, alerted by her tiny daughter's shouting, is quickly throwing a veil over her head before the visitors come in. She is very thin and looks drawn and tired but she smiles a welcome, waves aside Chandrakala's apologies, greets both of us and unfolds a mat and throws it on the floor, gesturing to us to sit.

Chandrakala declines and stands beside her, chatting. The little girl stands in front of me and shouts and points at the mat. I gesture towards Chandrakala and the door and say, '*Nahi – ne*,' but this only increases the volume of her outrage. I give in and sit down cross-legged.

The little girl folds her arms and stands there, watching me closely. The effect is of a sheepdog guarding a sheep with a tendency to bolt.

An older girl appears in the doorway but the mother says something to her and she quickly goes out again.

This is the poorest home I have so far seen – small and dark, like a barn, with a dirt floor and a tin roof held up by tree-trunk supports. The only air and light come in through gaps between the walls and the roof. The mat, some metal and plastic water barrels, metal cooking pots and a few bags hanging on hooks on the wall constitute the entire range of home comforts.

The older daughter returns now and shyly says hello. She is carefully carrying two bottles of ice-cold Pepsi with the tops just loosened, and hands one to me and the other to Chandrakala. I am both horrified – they can't afford it – and relieved, being really thirsty – and give Chandrakala a quick questioning look.

'I know,' she says quietly. 'But we have to accept; they'll be offended.'

She says something in Hindi and the older girl brings her a plastic beaker into which Chandrakala decants half her bottle of drink, but when I go to do the same, both she and the mother stop me.

'No, you drink,' Chandrakala says. So I thank them all in turn, including the little girl who is now beaming, and drink.

Chandrakala sits down on the mat beside me and the mother and teenage girl sit on the dirt floor. The little girl runs and sits on her mother's lap.

The father now comes in, greets us, and draws up a piece of furniture I hadn't noticed: a low stool made from a rectangle of laminated chipboard mounted on two strips of wood. He sits. There are now four pairs of eyes watching us.

What does everyone seem to be waiting for? The child's eyes are huge and luminous. The older girl looks, if anything, more exhausted than the mother. The father sits nodding and smiling but passive.

The mother says something to the older girl, who gets up and unhooks a bag hanging on the wall, takes something out of it and hands it to Chandrakala. It's an X-ray.

'It's the older daughter's,' Chandrakala tells me, translating as the mother tells her. 'There is something wrong with her chest – a constriction. The doctor doesn't know what it is, whether TB or some other thing.'

The elder girl has gone very still. There are dark circles under her eyes.

'How old is she?' I ask Chandrakala.

She checks with the mother. 'Fourteen.'

'What's her name?'

'Nadira.'

I think the name is Muslim but I don't know. I look at the X-ray and look at the faces and say, 'Can we pray with her?'

'I think so,' Chandrakala says. She asks the mother and the daughter, who immediately agree.

I ask the father, 'Is it OK with you?' and he nods and says yes.

I gesture to the mat and the girl comes and sits next to me. 'OK if I lay on hands?' I ask Chandrakala. 'Will she be comfortable with that?'

Another exchange. 'Yes.'

The little girl has left her mother's lap and is standing watching us again. I beckon her to come and help, and she half-sits, half-lies on the mat and takes her sister's hand.

Chandrakala leans forward and prays silently. I put one hand on the girl's back and the other on her near shoulder and begin to pray in tongues, as with Sharmila in the Aruna drop-in.

The girl is very tense. I think I have done the wrong thing, in suggesting this. She is paralyzed with fear. Is she afraid of me, a foreigner? She doesn't appear to be. I glance at her and she smiles encouragingly.

I have a sudden, icy memory of myself at fourteen. *I recognise this feeling. I lived like this, in fear, in a dangerous home environment. This is not how she's feeling at this moment. It's how she is. She is terrified. She has been this way for a long time.*

I have a mental image of this girl sleeping at night in a shack with not only no lock on the door but no door, in a district known for alcoholism and abuse, in a country plagued by human trafficking gangs, controlled only by police with limited resources, who sometimes turn a blind eye.

The phrase *'in fear of her life'* comes to mind. I say to Chandrakala, 'Shall we pray for her protection?' and she says, 'Yes, I think we should.'

We carry on praying for a little while, till Nadira relaxes and smiles.

'Tell Nadira we'll keep praying for her at home,' I ask, and Chandrakala relays this and says, 'We'll pray for her at the centre as well. I'll keep visiting them.'

The little girl jumps up and stands back, and starts shouting again. Everyone laughs.

'She says she is going to sing you a song,' Chandrakala says, and she proceeds to do so, loudly and gustily, flinging out her hands. At the end of it we all clap and she shouts again but her mother tells her to be quiet. Chandrakala says, 'She says she is going to sing another one, but we should go now.'

There is a slight altercation, followed by compromise.

'She will say a short poem.'

The child recites, with a few gaps to catch her breath or remember words, and we all clap again, then the mother takes hold of her firmly before she prolongs the concert.

But she is still singing after us as we make our way back down the alleyway.

I'm wondering who chooses to work in the slum – to take on a share of the often insoluble problems of people who don't come first on anyone's agenda? And how do they cope with their own stress, both in their personal lives and at work?

Back at the centre, Chandrakala introduces me to Ruth, 24, a nurse, and to Laxmi, 23, who taught *balwadi* and now trains women as pre-school teachers. Both have worked here for six years. As we sit down to talk, four young girls come in, run up the ladder to see who's there and run down again. The older girl shoos the other three out, but they come back and stand just inside the open metal shutter doorway and watch us. Two look like sisters, dressed in identical outfits, torn and missing buttons. They both look strained, the younger one as if about to cry. These children are not enjoying their childhood.

I ask Ruth what it's like working in the slum.

'This area is tough,' she says. 'There are some fears. Before joining, I worked here for one day and I said to God, "You have to change me, please, because I am not managing." To change the slum, I needed God to change me.'

'Did he change you?'

'Yes, for my good. Then I felt I could be of help here. When I visit the women I see they don't take care of themselves, only of the children. I tell them, if they are well educated themselves they can teach their family, and if they are healthy they can look after the kids. It's difficult to teach people to think differently. Self-confidence is necessary, in ourselves first. But we are also learning from them: how to exist. We want everything that's good, but they are happy with anything they have.'

Chandrakala confirms this. 'They are not looking for "good-better-best", but just doing what they can.'

I ask Chandrakala what brought her to work here. At 24, she has a degree in psychology and sociology; her college friends have office jobs earning four or five times the salary she receives.

'My friends say, "What are you doing here?!" but working in the community is a blessing from God for me. People should understand how life is: some people have many things but no contentment and some people are struggling just to live.'

'Do you see this as a long-term job?'

'It's important to stay, to build trust. I live very near the slum, so sometimes after work I meet people from here in the market. It's not that I am teacher and they are beneficiary, but now they are like good friends.'

Laxmi grew up in a slum and knows the problems first-hand. She says candidly that she had no intention of working in a slum but she knew God was calling her here.

'The people in community are hard. It takes a long time. You have to be willing to stay, to spend time with people, because they need it. You have to listen to their problems.'

'What's been the most difficult thing for all of you, working here?' I ask.

'I find it very hard to say no,' Chandrakala says, 'and when you help someone, sometimes their expectations go very high.'

Laxmi agrees. 'The women were expecting more things from us and we said, "We don't have anything; we are the same as you. I have time to spend with you; I can come with you wherever you want; I have ideas that can help, but I don't have money or any of the material things you want. But you think what you want to do, and we'll support you." And because we have a good relationship with them, they accept that now.'

'Has it worked the same way with people accepting you as Christians?'

As she talks, Chandrakala is sorting out the *balwadi* children's cupboard. She holds up a series of pictures of Noah's Ark, beautifully hand-drawn and painted.

'They're lovely. Where do they come from?'

'I did them for the children.'

Two giraffes with benign expressions oversee a procession of overweight rhinos, smiling elephants and a host of smaller creatures. Noah has a flowing white beard and appropriately dark skin. I tell her about Charmaine's set of Sunday school posters, with the white Hollywood-star Eve and Tarzan-style Adam. 'Charmaine would love these. Can you copy them?'

She laughs and puts them back in the cupboard. 'They're not good enough.'

She resumes, 'Initially, it was a problem to people that we were Christians; they thought we came to convert them. Oasis originally started *balwadi* in the temple place, which is an open space, and the Hindu people asked Kuldeep, the project organiser, "Bow down to our god and we'll let you use this place." But Kuldeep said, "No, we can't do that." So they wouldn't let us bring the children there. But suddenly, somehow God answered our prayers and we got this building here – very close to the temple, just behind the wall.' She smiles. 'We actually saw people who used to talk very harshly to us change and talk softly; now they trust us. It's a very small change, but very big too.'

When Chandrakala closes the Oasis centre for the day, by pulling down the metal shutter, we walk away from the slum, emerging into an area of no-man's-land, a stretch of dusty soil and rubble the width of a road, between pristine new apartment blocks and the slum. The windows of the apartments look out on to rusty sheets of corrugated iron settled loosely over the walls of shacks.

One family is camped out in the open, with lines of washing slung along the wall. Behind a hole in the wall is a tiny shop shaded by a tree. Bicycles are parked in the centre of the area, and rickshaws at the far end. Barefoot children play in the dust. One more block of apartments, in which these people would have no hope of living, would wipe out this whole area of street-level subsistence.

Further along, a group of men is gathered around a man swathed in white. He is standing with his back to us and two men are holding him by the arms. Two others are holding up a sheet behind him as a screen, concealing him from knee to waist level. They are in front of an open shack like a shop but it doesn't appear to be selling anything. On a sheet on the ground by his feet is a range of what look like surgical instruments. I look at Chandrakala and open my mouth to ask the question but she is looking straight ahead of her and walking fast.

John picks me up in the car; it's not really on his way but he's decided against a repeat of the taxi and motor-bike episode, which is a relief. On the way home, he says, 'What did you think of Bandra?'

I can't find the words. 'Extremely . . .'

He laughs. 'Quite.'

I tell him about the man behind the white sheet screen. 'What was that about?'

'I don't know! What do you think it was?'

'Street circumcision or something?'

'Eeugh!'

When we get home, Charmaine asks, 'How did you get on?'

'It was good. A good day.'

'You look tired. I bought you some Diet Coke; it's in the fridge. There's time for a shower if you want.' She's so nice. I'm about to hug her then realise it would be kinder if I had the shower first.

I don't see the cockroach till I open my eyes after rins-ing the shampoo out and catch a swift movement of something dark by my foot. They don't bite. Do they? I was going to run out of the shower at just that moment anyway. And it makes more sense to dry off in the bed-room, where the ceiling fan helps in the drying process. It's not that I'm scared of a tiny little huge black shiny cockroach or anything.

Chapter 11

Meeting a Career Man

Last night, in true British-visitor-to-India tradition, I got the runs and spent part of the night in the bathroom.

I wake in the morning with the ceiling fan whirring in the heat and my legs, still swollen, propped up on pillows, and know I am going to throw up if I move. So I stay still and pray and eventually go back to sleep.

Mid-morning, Charmaine comes in to see if I'm all right and asks if I need to see a doctor but I feel I'll be OK, so she makes me fresh lime juice with sugar and salt to prevent dehydration. I suspect she's also praying. After another sleep I feel better and get up to do some work on the computer, jotting down details of the projects and observations on Mumbai.

John phones to say that one of the young men he had in mind for me to interview could come out to the apartment as he lives in this area. This sounds an easy way to work so I sit back and wait to meet Rahul. Raju (Rahul to his friends) started life as a roadside dweller and was given training then a job with Oasis. Now, at 26, he is one of their trainers, helping others to leave street life behind them.

He arrives armed with apologies for his English. Charmaine offers to interpret from either Hindi or Marathi, as he's a local boy. But it's clear after a few sentences that his English is very good and Rahul is naturally articulate, so Charmaine brings him a cold drink and leaves him to it.

'Where shall I begin my story?' he asks.

'As far back as you like.'

'Then I think I have to begin before I came in this world – when I was in my mother,' Rahul says thoughtfully.

'My mum had three daughters and she was waiting for a son. I come from a Hindu background and it's very important to Hindus to have a son, so when my third sister was born she was disappointed.

'When she was expecting me, she was thinking about abortion. She didn't want to be disappointed again. So she took many medicines, but the abortion didn't happen.'

Hang on.

'How did you come to know about this – that your mother tried to abort you?'

'My mum told me this recently,' he says, smiling disarmingly.

'How did you feel about that, Rahul?'

'I was very happy when she told me.'

'*Happy?*'

'Yes, because I thought, "Maybe God has some plan for me. Maybe it's a sign, that I lived when my mum took so many drugs."'

Wow. How's that for a positive take on negative circumstances?

'Did you have an idea of what the plan might be?' I ask him.

'I thought I ought to go into the church, for ministry. But I didn't have a good beginning to my life. My whole family lived on the street – building roads. They worked very, very hard.'

These are the people I've seen, the families living in rubble beside a half-made road, carrying rocks on their heads all day, assisted by very young children. They are the very thin people living in shelters made from plastic sheets, separate from the community.

'What was it like, living on the roadside?'

'We had very bad conditions in the home,' says Rahul. The smile goes out of his eyes. 'We couldn't get good food. My two older sisters even had to beg and ask neighbours for money. So my mum decided to send my younger sister and me to the government hostel.[8] I was there from eight to eighteen – First to Eighth Standard at school. I came home in Standard Nine and stayed at school to Standard Twelve.

'My family speaks the Marathi language and I had been in Marathi-speaking classes up till then, but I couldn't get a place in the Marathi class when I came home. So I had to take the exams in Hindi and I failed in the Twelfth Standard and my mum said I had to find a job. I tried for six months to get a job in an office, or packing. I was very upset with myself, that I couldn't get anything.'

'What was it like in the hostel, living away from home?'

'There was food, and an education,' he says philosophically. 'It was not a Christian hostel but when I was there, in Eighth Standard, they showed us a film about Jesus. I didn't understand it but when I saw him die on the cross, I cried. And one time a woman came from Germany and shared with us about the gospel, and I knew that this Jesus was God. I didn't believe in other gods, Hindu gods. This lady also gave us a Bible.

'I wanted to know how to be a good man. One day I was reading the Bible by myself, a part that said that a man who lives for God will be ridiculed – and some friends came along just then and ridiculed me for reading the Bible!'

'Were you taught about the Hindu faith as well?'

'Yes. And I studied Jesus, and the Indian gods, for myself. The Hindu gods are lovable but also they are cruel and in their hands they carry swords and axes. But God just spoke and it happened. And Jesus was like this: he spoke and things happened as he said. So this was my logic and I felt really happy, that Jesus is real. But it's hard to live as a good man. In Tenth Standard, I was thinking, "I have very bad friends. If I want to walk with the Lord I have to be with his people only, then I won't go up and down."

'I asked God: "Give me a good job with people who love you, because I'm afraid I won't walk with you if I'm with people who don't." A friend told me that some training is going on at Oasis but it is only for street children with no education. He told me to tell lies because if I said I had been educated up to Twelfth Standard, even though I had failed, they wouldn't take me. I had to pray and ask the Lord, "What is your desire?" I went to the training centre and met Sucheta, who was the project director at the time, and Saby, the trainer. They interviewed me and I decided to tell them the truth about my education and my background. Then she started shouting at me, "You have a good education; why do you come here?"

'I said it was very true and I didn't know why I came! I explained that for six months I couldn't get any job and I was frustrated. Then she said they would help me: I could come for one year's training, not two years like the others. They put me on a screen-printing course and I had six months there, but in that time I learned so many things, especially spiritual things – that God is a real God, and how he loves us. Everybody prayed together and I liked that. I saw that in Oasis everybody was a believer. It was what I had prayed for, so I asked the Lord, "Put me here and make me strong in you."

'After six months I changed to the electrician course. After two months, Sucheta called me and said, "Would you like to work with us?" She offered me the office assistant job and I worked in the main office of Oasis for one and a half years. On my first day there, John asked me to bring something but he spoke in Hindi and I'd never heard an English person speak Hindi before, so I just stood there with my mouth open, and John said, "Raju, I'm speaking to you!"

'Saby had been my trainer when I was a trainee. And all the time I was working in the office, I felt God tell me, "I will put Saby up and give you his job and take you back in the training centre." I never forgot that vision, even through one and a half years. I was waiting for it and asked God to take me fast.'

'Did you like the office job?'

'Mmm.'

I get the impression he's being diplomatic.

'Not really?'

'In the office I was making tea and washing the plates and I felt it wasn't my calling. After one and a half years I was very upset and I decided to find a new job and I wrote out my history, but then Vasu came from the training centre and asked me if I'd like to come back to the centre as a trainer, not a trainee! So I came as a trainer in screen-printing.'

'How long ago was that, Rahul?'

'Now one and a half years I am there. I am really very happy because I feel it's God's work and I want to work in his kingdom. Sanjiv, the project co-ordinator, is teaching me a lot of things on the computer, and to do paperwork. The need for money is always there and more can be earned in other places but I don't think about salary and I don't feel I should go and find a new job. You need something for food, but when my mum shared with me about the abortion then I came to see God has some plan for me, and he answered my prayer to work only with believers and he put me on the training list. So I am asking for another sign, for God's next step. Wherever he wants to take me, I will go there.'

'What would you say to people in other countries, like the UK, who have easier lives and more money and want to know how to find peace?'

Rahul thinks for a minute, revolving the empty plastic beaker in his hands carefully. 'When I came to know God,' he says, 'I knew no one can love like him, without any reason. Ask the Lord, "Why do you love me so much?" and he says, "Because I made you." If I made this glass, I would take very good care of it and I wouldn't like it if anyone put any less value on it. God wouldn't want anyone to put anything less on us. He loves us just as we are.

'Man's thinking and God's thinking are very different: man has this tiny mind and our definition of love is very small. God's love is very different: you can feel that, but you can't give a definition. You can just feel, and it's very sweet: you can just taste. Sometimes I ask, "Just give me that bite!"'

He goes silent, thinking about this, and I guess the interview is ended. We subside into chat about this and that and he relaxes. I tell him about the churches at home, and about my meeting with Pastor Thomas, and he says, 'We believe in miracles. My sister was healed by a miracle.'

I reach for the notebook again. 'Oh, right? So you didn't think to mention this tiny detail? Spill it!'

He laughs, and spills.

'When I was home after the hostel, in Ninth Standard, my elder sister got a stomach tumour. It was big – you could see it and feel it. My mum took her to hospital – very far from Thane – and the doctor said she had to have an operation and set her an admission date. But when they went there, the hospital was on strike. They came home and at Bandrup station there was a crusade meeting going on. My mum was a very new believer and I never went to church then. The pastor didn't know us but he told us to go to the meeting and God would heal my sister. So my whole family decided we should go there.

'We arrived late and it had already started. They were asking anyone who had AIDS or cancer or anything to come to the stage, and they prayed. But my sister was standing back and wouldn't go; she was feeling shy and we were very new: we didn't know Jesus was a healer, only that he died. I told her to go; something would happen. So she went near the stage and the pastor was praying, "Lord, heal them." After a minute it was very quiet. The pastor said, "Whoever feels their sickness is gone, come on the stage and give testimony," and I saw my sister on the stage and she said, "I had a tumour I could feel in my hand and now it's gone."

'When my sister came back we asked her, "Is it really gone?" and she said, "Touch it and feel that it's gone." And she said, "Somebody touched me – like a human touch." It's eight years ago now and she's well.'

Charmaine returns at this stage to see how the interview's going and if we need more drinks. I ask Rahul to tell her about the miracle he didn't think was worth mentioning. He tells her in Hindi, then they have a brief conversation in Marathi.

'Rahul has another miracle he didn't mention,' Charmaine says, and he tells me this one too before he leaves.' My father had epileptic fits and he was having a fit one day when the pastor called by and prayed for him and he hasn't had another fit since – seven years. But he still drinks,' he adds sadly, 'so we are still praying for him.'

Chapter 12

House of Wholeness

Robin phoned last night and told me the cat was dead.

I'm upset but feel I'm hardly entitled to be over the loss of a family pet, when there are families here, such as Rahul's, unable to feed their children and forced to send them away to make sure they survive. And there are children here grieving at losing parents to the terrible epidemic that is AIDS.

Today I'm going to visit Purnata Bhavan – House of Wholeness – the home for women and children affected by AIDS. Some children are orphaned by it though not infected themselves. Others are with their mothers who are HIV Positive. Many children are Positive themselves. The home is a two-hour drive out of Mumbai, in a rural spot far from all the pollution – and the facilities – of the city.

I ask John about the scale of the HIV problem in India. In the UK the headlines have been about AIDS in Africa. How many people are affected here?

'A higher percentage than anyone expected,' John says. 'About two people in every hundred have HIV. With the tradition of virginity before marriage it was expected to be lower. It took time to trace one of the major causes of the spread of the disease to another tradition – temple prostitution. It's a centuries-old practice but no one had realised quite how prevalent. It turns out to have been a strong factor in the spread of AIDS in India.'

On the journey to Purnata Bhavan, we pass small clusters of houses constructed from tree branches, with goats and chickens wandering around in the dusty red soil. Some villages have a well, wide-mouthed and open, unlike the pitched-roof traditional wells that survive or are replicated in villages at home. Even with a lot of irrigation, I can't imagine what would grow easily here. There doesn't seem to be much tender vegetation. Like people, only the wiry varieties survive.

'What do people live on?' I ask John.

'Some of them go into the city to work. Otherwise, it's a very difficult life.'

I think of the people living by the roadside, deprived of privacy, fresh air and security. With all the risks to their health and life in Mumbai, do they still have more chance of survival there than scratching a living in the dust of their native villages where the air is purer and they're part of the natural environment and a community?

The road climbs up some steep mountainsides. There haven't been any villages now for miles.

'What would you do if the car broke down?'

'I used to go everywhere by motorbike and it was always breaking down!' John says. 'If you're in the middle of nowhere, there's not much you can do.'

I'm beginning to understand reliance on God as the means to survive, not an optional concept. Several times now on this trip, I've felt as though God was nudging me: 'Now will you rely *only* on me?'

So what does that mean I usually rely on? I may *feel* more confident in a familiar environment, within reach of people I can call on in case of need, but that's surely a false security and a barrier to achieving real security by relying on God? It's a very different perspective from self-help, self-sufficiency, 'believe it, want it, have it' psychologies, or even 'getting in touch with your inner power' or 'trusting the universal power' or 'higher power' or 'energy'. With God, it's personal. It has to be.

The car turns off the empty highway and down a road of compacted soil and loose gravel. A weather-beaten sign announces that we are entering the domain of Purnata Bhavan, a project of Oasis India, care community for women and children who are infected or affected by HIV/AIDS. It adds a quote – an ambitious and breathtakingly un-self-protective promise: *Jesus said, 'Come to me, all you who are tired and are carrying heavy loads. I will give you rest.'*

Flat, scrubby brown fields flank the soil road. A low mountain rises in the distance. Overhead cables lead the eye to a cluster of young trees surrounding a group of pleasantly designed two-storey buildings with pitched roofs, and a round tower. A new building is under construction and, beside a playground with slides, swings and a rope climbing-frame, a truck is unloading heaps of red soil. Flower beds containing small trees, shrubs and succulent plants are edged with low hedging. In its rather barren environment, the place looks lovingly planned and cared for, and surprisingly sophisticated in contrast to Oasis' centres in Mumbai.

We get out of the car and are met by Prakash, a man of about forty, whom John introduces as co-manager of Purnata Bhavan, along with his wife Sujata who will be along later. Prakash shakes hands and walks us round the building work, explaining the progress. There are three residential buildings here, each with house-parents. 'But we are one community,' he says.

A community that is outgrowing its present facilities, evidently.

'What's this being used for?' John asks, indicating the heaps of soil by the playground.

'The soil left from the work will make a bigger playground. We will get more play equipment.'

A dog with seven large puppies comes up. That's a lot of dogs. *Lord, I've done the dog-fear one; didn't you tick it off the list? The packs of strays in Mumbai and around the apartment car park – don't they count?* Obviously not. The puppies are jumping up at us and trying to nibble my ankles. I shuffle away surreptitiously and they follow, delighted with the moving feet.

'They're cute,' John says. 'The kids must love them.'

Prakash laughs. 'They all like different ones. They want to keep them all!'

'How many will you keep?' John asks him.

'Oh – we'll have to keep them all, I think!' *Good father.* The phrase pops unbidden into my mind. Growing up as a fatherless child, I used to rate friends' fathers on their ability to see life from a child's point of view rather than from a self-important height. Prakash scooped the coveted Good Father award with that last remark.

Unconscious of the accolade, he leads us into the furthest building and points out the downstairs rooms occupied by some of the women, and upstairs rooms full of bunks.

Large windows let in the air and light, the curtains are bright and animal-patterned, and a large stuffed lion sprawls on one of the bunks. The dormitory walls are painted with underwater scenes featuring smiling whales, seahorses and imaginative varieties of fish.

'It needs repainting,' John comments.

The pictures are faded but still full of charm. In one corner, a verse from the psalms is written: *If I make my bed in the depths, you are there.*

'We will have to repaint it sometime,' agrees Prakash, 'but the outside needs doing first. We are getting quotes.'

'Wouldn't volunteers do this?' I ask. I can think of school-leavers at home who would love to come here for a month to build playgrounds and paint murals. Prakash and John look doubtful.

'We don't get many volunteers out here,' Prakash says. 'We'd love to have more but we're rather far from the town. We do have three gap-year girls but they are mainly teaching the younger children.'

'How many children live here?' I ask him.

'At the moment we have 39.'

We hear the younger children singing as we pass another building. Various staff walk by and say hello but the older children are all at school in the morning. In the main building, a staircase leads up from a spotlessly clean hall with shining tile floor, where small tables are set end to end with plastic stools alongside them. In the kitchen, glimpsed through the open door, two women in saris are sitting on the floor making *chapattis*.

On our way to meet Sujata, Prakash's wife, John becomes aware of a small face looking down at us over the top of the brick-sided staircase.

'Arun,' he calls, 'what are you doing off school?'

The face disappears, then reappears grinning, and a small boy runs down the stairs, clad in oversized denim shorts, polo shirt and flip-flops. He starts talking in Hindi but when John says, 'Speak in English because you're good at it,' he switches effortlessly. 'Why are you at home today?' John asks him again.

The child points to a row of raised spots above one eyebrow. It doesn't look very serious.'A mosquito came in the night and bite me,' he says. He has a wide smile and the eyes of an old man, sad and wise.

'Are you taking anything for this?' John asks him.

'Yes, I have pills and I will have cream.' I realise suddenly that this is serious. A child with HIV has very low immunity. Even an insect bite could get infected and affect his health significantly.

John sits on a bench and Arun stands and chats to him, man to man, leaning comfortably. The child has dark circles under his eyes and looks small for his age – eight, John tells me – but his eyes are bright and he talks animatedly. After a while he runs off to the kitchen to talk to the women.

We walk over to the office, in a smaller building, which has two desks shared among staff, a row of chairs, and a sink that fills from an urn and empties into a plastic dustbin. Sujata, a welcoming and articulate woman in her thirties, offers to take me to see the training work and craft activities and to meet the people who have agreed to tell me about themselves.

We go over to another building with small rooms on the ground floor which are accommodation for some of the women and for the three British gap-year girls. I haven't seen all the children yet but these three residential units suggest occupation by a large number of people. As we move on, I ask Sujata, 'Where do you and your family live?'

'In the building we were just in, upstairs. We'll go there afterwards. This room up here is for Aari work. The women come in from the villages to learn skills, as well as the ones who live here.'

I recognise the work from the Vocational Training Centre: the canvas stretched over a horizontal frame like a bed frame. Two women are sitting on cushions on the floor, stitching beads on to embroidered flowers, a small heap of beads between them on the frame and bottles of drinking water beside them on the floor. They smile and show their work, which is beautiful.

'They are just learning,' Sujata says. 'We're hoping to start selling more work commercially, as we do with the tailoring. And the candles we make here as well. We have groups of visitors coming round the place and they often ask if they can buy them. Madhukshi is in charge of this.'

We go into a workshop where Madhukshi and a shy young trainee, wearing aprons over their *shalwar kameez*, demonstrate the wax melting in the pans and the moulds for making candles. There is a peaceful atmosphere.

'Madhukshi is going to come and talk to you,' Sujata says. 'Will you be able to leave the work for a while, Madhukshi?' She repeats this in Hindi, and Madhukshi nods and smiles. She has an amazing smile; her whole being shines. She is wearing bright blue with a white embroidered neckline and looks plump and healthy and at ease with herself.

As we go downstairs, Sujata says, 'She has an amazing history. She lost both her children and her husband and she has the virus herself.'

'She looks fantastic!'

'She is. She has a very strong faith.'

The children are coming back from school as we go out of the building. The place is suddenly full of activity and exuberant shouting. Arun runs out of the kitchen and is greeted by three small boys, who drop their schoolbags and rush off beyond the trees with him.

'They've gone to chase cows out of the orchard,' Sujata says. 'They make it their job!'

Cows are not sacred, then, in this Christian territory. It must be a shock to be chased by four young boys who don't recognise the divinity of the orchard-raiders.

'I want you to meet Esther, Arun's older sister,' Sujata says. 'The children lost both their parents to AIDS.'

We go back into the hall with the dining tables and Esther comes in, a girl who looks about fifteen but who, like her brother, has the eyes of someone who has seen more of life than many adults.

I explain to her that I'm writing for people who may not be familiar with Indian culture or with the kind of lives people here live, and that it would be good to hear her story but only if she's happy to tell it.

She nods.

'I am willing to tell you,' she says.

Chapter 13

The Breadwinner

'You might be surprised to know that I am twenty,' Esther begins.

I am surprised. I had thought she was fifteen, or seventeen at the most.

'I am in my last year at school. I'm head girl. My brother Kumar is fifteen and is at boarding school, and my younger brother Arun is eight and living here at Purnata Bhavan with me, but they only keep boys here till they are twelve or thirteen. I was born in Bombay. I went to school but when I was nine, I had some financial problems at home so I left school and started working, and I worked till fourteen years old.'

'What work did you do, Esther?'

She hesitates.

'You don't have to tell me anything you don't want to,' I remind her.

'If you don't mind, I don't think I will say this,' she says awkwardly.

'That's OK. Sorry – go on.'

'On 4th August 2000 I came here, and within three months my mother died, and then twenty days after that my father died. I didn't know they were going to die. But the night before, it came into my heart that they would die. This happened before, and it has happened four times now: first my mum and then my dad, then a girl here, then another girl.'

'How did you feel about knowing they were going to die?'

'I am afraid,' she says.

Present tense. I don't think that's an accident. Her English is accomplished.

'Why are you afraid?' I ask.

She has an air of quiet dignity, this girl, but her hands have tensed and her eyes behind her glasses look troubled. 'Because I don't want to lose people. I was very upset that I could see them in my mind, dead, while they were still alive. I asked God why this happened and said I didn't want it. I thought it was my fault, that I'd done something wrong.'

'You thought you were causing it in some way?'

'Somebody told me it was the devil acting in me.'

Her hands are twisting together and she looks down at them.

'Somebody here told you that?' I ask.

'No. At school. I prayed but it didn't go away. Also when I saw one of my aunties I felt, "I won't see her again." I still kept praying for her but she lived for two days and then died.'

'Were all these people expected to die? Were they ill or did it happen suddenly?'

'No, they were all ill but no one knew when they would die. But I saw them dead and then they died.' She seems on the point of tears now. I forget the interview.

'Listen,' I say. 'You're not causing people to die.'

'I don't know,' she says, unconvinced.

'I do know of other people who have this ability to see something before it happens,' I tell her. 'It's considered a gift from God, but it is a difficult one to have and most people who have it would rather they didn't.'

She looks up. 'I certainly don't see it as a gift!' she says.

'No. If it's frightening you, then ask God to take it back.'

She frowns. 'Why would it be a gift?'

'It could be your mind letting you know something in advance – something that's going to happen anyway, not something you've caused or something you could prevent.'

She thinks about this.

'If you didn't have this vision of the person dying,' I say, 'they would die anyway and someone would come and tell you when it happened. It would still be a shock, wouldn't it?'

'Yes.'

'But if you'd prefer it that way, then ask God to take away the vision. He doesn't want us to have any gift that we don't want.'

Her head is down but her hands have gone still.

'I think I will keep it,' she says. She is silent for a minute then looks up and says, 'Thank you for telling me this.'

'Are you OK?'

'Yes, I am OK, thanks. Shall I go on telling you about my family?'

'Please.'

She collects her thoughts and resumes, sitting upright and speaking clearly. 'My brother Arun was just two at the time when my parents died. I had a big dream for him, that I would teach him and he would have a good chance in life, but I was only in Fifth Standard, so I wasn't able to. Then I find he is HIV Positive. I didn't have any knowledge about it and I thought, "I will work and earn money and he will get well."

'I took care of him and I took him to hospital, and from there I heard there is a home over here. Two people told me about this home and I am afraid that they will

use me or take me to some wrong place. So first of all I
said no. But when I came here I saw them all pray.'

'What did you think about that?'

'I knew these people were good then so it was all right
to come here to live. I had no job here and they asked me
if I want to go to school. By then I believed in Jesus and
I decided I did want to go to school, because I prayed
about it. So at the end of September I started school, after
four and a half years away from it.'

'Was that hard, going back to school after such a long
gap?'

'I failed in the first exams,' Esther says, 'especially
English and science. But in the next exams I got sixty
percent.'

'Wow.'

'God helped me,' she says.

'And I guess you worked!'

She smiles. 'Well, yes, I worked hard as well! But I
asked him to help. In Sixth Standard, age fifteen, I
prayed, "Lord, I want to be a prefect in Ninth Standard."
I asked for Ninth but got it in Eighth! Then I prayed to
be head girl in Tenth Standard and I got it in Ninth!'

'What job would you like to get?' I ask her.

She hesitates again. 'I'd like to do a medical course
and get the degree of Doctor. But what I hear in my heart
is, "Go, tell it on the mountain." This message I got the
first year here in camp. My faith became very strong at
that time. It was difficult for me because I wanted to be
with all the girls; I was fifteen and wanted to enjoy
myself but I had to look after my brother.'

'After you came here? You didn't have to look after
him all the time then, did you?'

She shakes her head, agreeing, but looks doubtful.
'When my brother became sick I felt very bad that I
didn't do more for him before,' she explains.

'Do you have plans – ideas of how you'd like your life to go from here?' I ask.

Her answer is not what I expect.

'I want to take baptism soon. One lady came from the UK and she prayed over us. I had been praying to talk in tongues and have baptism in the Holy Spirit, and when she prayed over me I started speaking in tongues. Sometimes I get touched by God and I feel very cool and relaxed. I have prayer time every day here but we have special prayer meetings when people are sick, and sometimes outside people come and pray for us. I saw some people who came translate visions and so on, and I tell God, "I want that too!"'

I think these must be the groups of visitors Sujata mentioned, who come from different churches, sometimes from abroad, to see the work here and contribute whatever they have to give, including praying for the children when they return home.

Having visions seems an unusual ambition for a twenty-year old girl, especially one afraid of the foresight she'd had of her parents' deaths.

'Tell me about this desire to be a doctor,' I ask her. 'Where did that come from?'

'From when I was first going to school,' she says. 'I saw beggars on the road and they had boils and some were bleeding, and I saw some people on the railway station and in the hospital, and I felt that people need doctors who are devoted to them, and I saw some doctors who are careless. But when I left school at nine years old, I thought I won't be able to be a doctor, so I'll make my brother a doctor – but he wants to become a pilot!

'When my mother was ill I had to travel one hour from my home and go to the hospital and take my brother, to see my mother. Children were not allowed in the ward because it was a TB hospital, so I had to leave

Arun in the canteen. The fellows there were good and would look after him while I'd go up to see my mother.

'I used to pay money for that; they didn't ask for it, but I did because it was right. Then I would see my mother. There was no one with her; I had to see what the doctor said and do what she needed. My father was sick at home. So I had to look after my father, mother and brother. I said, "I will work hard but I will never, *never* beg."'

She pauses, then comes to a decision.

'OK, I will tell you what kind of work I did. My job was selling articles on local trains.'

I think of the little girls going up and down the trains illegally selling hair slides and beads. I was expecting worse when Esther was reluctant to tell me, but this work after all is not far away from the begging she sees as shameful, and for a shy child it must have brought a sense of dread.

'When I was doing this work I had many friends and they were kind to me. One of my girl-friends wanted to take me somewhere; she told me, "This is my boy-friend," then a few days later there was another man and she told me, "This is my boyfriend now." She wanted me to come with her, but another friend told me, "Esther, don't go; she's not a good girl." So I kept a distance from her.'

'It must have been frightening,' I suggest, 'having to work on the trains?'

'At first I was very frightened,' she admits. 'I couldn't travel without my parents. But my brother Kumar told me, "Go on, we can do this." He had run away from home twice; he used to make mistakes and get beatings from Dad, so he ran.'

'You said he was at boarding school? Do you get to see him?'

'I see him about every six months. I'm upset that he's living away but when he was here, we were fighting every day so perhaps it is best. But Arun is with me; he listens to me and he loves me.'

She goes quiet again and her head sinks low. Her hands are twisting again. I think of Arun, chasing cows in the orchard with his friends, but also think of the dark shadows round the old-man's eyes in the thin little face, and being kept home from school for mosquito bites.

'Are you worried about Arun?' I ask Esther, as gently as possible.

She tightens her lips. 'Arun's cell count is very low now,' she says. 'It's not good for the count to go down so low, and sometimes things go very wrong. I told them here which medicine to give him because I know which works but they wait till they take him to the doctor. Sometimes dressings need changing every day but they leave it two or three days.'

I wonder if Esther finds it difficult, having had to assume the parental role for so long towards both her parents and her small brother, to let others take over that role now. But she knows Arun better than anybody and watches him closely and if she thinks he could be getting better treatment, it must be agony to watch him and say nothing.

'Have you told someone you don't feel your brother's getting the best treatment?'

'No. I don't like to make complaints.' She hesitates then says, 'I will have to talk to someone. I know how to look after Arun. He had scabs over his eyes and I had to clean them every day and pus used to come out and he used to cry. We stayed in hospital fifteen days and I am doing everything for my brother, and the doctors said he could go home. When he got better we went to one of the families, church members, who take people for holidays, so we had a holiday and they were very kind.'

'Do you have other family, Esther?'

'I have an uncle and aunty in Canada and they came to see me and they phone now. But they gave Arun *prasad*[9] and I told him not to eat it because it has been used to worship idols, but he was young so he didn't understand.'

'Do you feel that the people here at Purnata Bhavan are your family now who will help look after Arun, or do you feel responsible for Arun yourself still?'

'We have a saying, "Our blood is our blood; others' blood is water." He's my brother, so I take care of him,' Esther says. 'Some children at school ask me questions about HIV and is my brother positive? Now some people know and there is gossip. The teachers asked me if all the children from here were positive, and I said, "I don't know." I can talk about myself, but I won't talk about the others.'

'Is there any prejudice from the parents of other children at the school?'

'Sometimes they give the small children chocolate and ask them questions about Purnata Bhavan, so I told them if they have questions, ask the Purnata Bhavan staff. So I don't allow any of our children to go with any parents.'

'You feel responsible for the other children here, as well as for Arun?'

'It's my responsibility to take care of them,' Esther says. 'Other children used to stare at them, so I tell them to come and play with me at break-time, and my friends are good. At first they were not friends; they said, "Why are you living at that place for people with AIDS if you don't have it?" I told them, "So what if I am living with HIV/AIDS people; where else will I live? Will you give me education and feed and clothe me and take me in your home?" So later they changed their attitude and became very nice to me.'

She is brave, this girl, standing up for herself and defending her brother and all the other children as well. But a phrase she used when she spoke about Arun's health resounds with me: *I feel very scared from inside.* Just about Arun, or about herself?

'Do you have any fear about moving on – leaving school, going on to adult life?'

'I do feel fear inside but God is training me,' she says. 'I have my ambition to become a doctor but in the end I say, "God, you do it your way, because if I do it my way it will go wrong." I feel God will take me where he wants; doors will open for me.'

She has gone quiet again. Noises and delicious smells from the kitchen suggest that it is nearly time for lunch.

'Is there anything else you'd like to say?' I ask Esther, and she smiles suddenly, confident.

'No, I think that is all I want.'

John comes in and chats to the children and the women for a while, then we go back to the office for him to make some phone calls. I take the opportunity to tell him about Esther's fear that Arun's symptoms are not always being dealt with quickly enough.

'I don't know if that's right or if it's just hard for her to hand over the parent role.'

'Either way, that's a major worry for her,' John says, 'and she needs to talk it over with somebody. I'll have a word with Sujata. Arun is one of four children we have on anti-retroviral drugs, which cost Oasis quite a lot of money every month but they seem to be helping them resist infection. Arun isn't doing so well as the other three, though. How did the interview go, otherwise?'

'She's an amazing girl. A lot of courage.'

'She is amazing. Are you going to meet Madhukshi?'

'I met her briefly in the candle-making room and Sujata says she is willing to be interviewed.'

'Good. We'll get some lunch first. How's your stomach?'

'Fine.' It's been churning like a washing machine but the run-resist tablets I swallowed last night seem to be working and the constant bathroom trips are not being repeated in the daytime.

I know people at home are praying for me to be healthy while I'm here, knowing physical stamina isn't my forte, and I also have a strong sense of Charmaine praying for me during each of these days visiting the projects.

I've asked if I can go with her to her cell group tonight – a small group of people from local churches who meet once a week for Bible study and to pray for each other.

John finishes making phone calls and we go back to the bigger building where the staff are now sitting at the tables having their lunch. I see Madhukshi and she smiles and pulls a wry face. It is nerve-racking to be interviewed, when the story is so personal.

John has said that Oasis doesn't allow visitors to question beneficiaries about their personal stories. If fund raisers or journalists ask for case histories, the names are always changed and they don't get to meet the individuals personally, to ensure the person's privacy.

I'm aware of being in a privileged position, and that the person who volunteers or agrees to be interviewed is taking a risk. Recalling where they've come from and seeing how far they've come may be therapeutic, but it can also be upsetting. I don't want to upset anyone. But all these personal stories are also the wider story of human beings trying to survive emotionally, physically and spiritually, in a world that can be hostile.

And if some people can survive such stresses as abuse, abandonment, destitution, human trafficking or losing their parents to AIDS, then there's surely something we can learn from them about surviving the stresses of everyday living.

I'm interested to talk to Madhukshi, who looks as though she is not only surviving but shining.

Chapter 14

Visionaries and Missionaries

Madhukshi is prepared. She doesn't need questions and only occasionally waits to be prompted to go on. We're sitting on one side of the desk in a small office next to the sewing workroom, with a cool air fan. Sujata sits on the other side of the desk, interpreting.

'I come from a Maharashtran family,' Madhukshi begins. 'My mum committed suicide because my father was an alcoholic. I have two brothers and one sister; I am the eldest. Because of the family problems I got married to Munjal; after two years we had a daughter but we were not aware of the virus: Munjal was HIV Positive. When our daughter was a year old we had a son and he was positive, so that's when we found out my husband was positive. My son died in one and a half months.'

I wait here for her reaction but there is none. She is concentrating on telling the facts. Unlike Sharmila at the day centre beside the brothel, though, Madhukshi doesn't give the impression of a tide of grief suppressed.

She is talking as though she has moved beyond these events and it was a long time ago. It can't have been that long, though. She is only 25.

'Then my husband died,' Madhukshi continues. 'He was in a state of shock after the baby and started losing his health, and when he saw his child die he became ill and died in two years. The family never accepted the marriage because it was a love match, not arranged. So there was no support from family after my husband died. I worked as a maid till my daughter was four, then she had an epileptic stroke and I couldn't leave her by herself, so she was in hospital for a long time.

'I met someone in the hospital who prayed with me and gave me the gospel, and another man had a child admitted and we became friends. I accepted this person as a brother. He helped me financially and gave me money to start a small business making poppadoms, frying and selling them, but it didn't make enough money. When my daughter came out of hospital she was totally dependent on me. By then I knew that both my daughter and I were HIV Positive. The neighbours wouldn't talk to me. No one knew whether I was in my home or not.'

This phrase is poignant. In the communities I've seen, a person's home is not their exclusive territory. People live in close proximity and women are in and out of each other's homes. For Madhukshi to say, 'No one knew whether I was in my home or not,' means she was rejected by the whole of her immediate society.

She goes on: 'Then the man helped me contact an NGO called Sati, and they referred me to Oasis. In 2002 I came to Purnata Bhavan. My daughter was fine for four months after we came here but then started getting epileptic attacks again and was bedridden for eight months. She was about five months in hospital, then the doctors gave up on her; she lost her voice and couldn't move.'

There is an infinitesimal pause before she continues.

'In January 2004, I lost my daughter.'

I am on the edge of tears here. Madhukshi smiles at me, and gives me a moment to recover before she goes on with her story.

'Before I came here I started to pray, and my faith increased as I started to pray for things. I had no money in my hand one day and my daughter was hungry and someone had told me, "You can pray if you need anything." So I prayed and this brother just happened to visit me and gave 500 rupees to my daughter. So then I prayed to go to some place to learn tailoring and be a teacher: that was my dream.'

'How did you feel when you first came to Purnata Bhavan?'

'I was quite frightened to be in an institution,' she says, 'but when I saw the place and my room and the tailoring class, I knew it was God. After the two years tailoring training here, I didn't know where I was going to go. Oasis staff saw I was able to teach the other girls with me and explain when they didn't understand, so they sent me for one month's training in the Vocational Training Centre.

'In July 2005 I came on the Oasis payroll. Now I train the women from the local villages in tailoring in the afternoons. I'm also training another girl here and helping in the candle production. My faith in God increased because I was exercising it in small things: I prayed, "God, take me to a place where I can learn." I started believing in the dreams I got and the changes that happened in my life: when I pray I expect something to happen.'

'Has it changed you?' I ask Madhukshi. 'All this suffering?'

'I have changed,' she agrees. 'I used to be a very possessive person; I always wanted things. But when I left home I gave away everything I had. I didn't want to possess things because God gives me everything I need, and I have learned to share.'

'You gave everything away?'

'Yes. When I knew I was going to come here, I thought, "I won't need all these things."'

'Who did you give them to?' I ask.

'To the neighbours.'

'You gave all your prized possessions to the neighbours who called you diseased and didn't care if you were at home or not?'

She laughs. 'They still needed these things and I didn't. I knew I was going to be cared for. I have changed in other ways. In difficult decisions, I go to God and he gives me dreams and answers and I don't worry.'

'What kind of dreams?' I wonder if this is anything like Esther's premonitions of people dying.

'Before Oasis sent me for training, I had a dream,' Madhukshi says. 'I dreamed that I had gone for training: I saw the Training Centre and I even saw the trainer's face, and a very cramped apartment where they trained people, and I saw the local trains in Mumbai and a bus from the station (which Oasis has) and God said to me, "I am going to send you there." And when I went there, everything was exactly as it was in the dream.

'In the dream also I saw a marketplace where I had no money to buy and just used to go with the other girls to see, and that happened too; we used to go there. In another dream I saw Prakash and people from different countries, as well as from the south of India, in a room. Every year Oasis has a staff conference and there's a chance for new staff to go and meet people, and when I went there the rooms were exactly as I saw in the dream, and the people's faces.'

'Do you think you would have been scared to go to these new places if you hadn't seen them first?'

'Yes, I would have been. It was very new to me, to be with all these kinds of people. But God showed it to me, so I wasn't scared when I went there.'

'Madhukshi, you've been through some incredibly difficult things. What would you say to us in Western countries, where life is so much easier and yet most people don't have that peace and happiness that you seem to have achieved?'

She thinks for a minute, then says, 'What I would say to other people is: people with HIV can be happy. There is hope especially for those who know Christ. He has given me hope and so much help to live my life – and I can live my life; I don't have to live to die. For Christians in countries where people have so much: obviously if people have everything they are not going to think about God, because they have so many things.' For the first time in her whole narrative, she looks sad.

'But if they share with others who don't have so much,' she goes on, 'if they can look into people's lives who don't have that bare minimum, then peace will come into them.'

'I guess if anyone else said that, it would sound like preaching,' I tell her. 'You're the only one who can tell us that, because you've actually done it.'

She smiles, and the room lights up. Malini, who has come to stand in the doorway and is watching us, starts smiling too. It's contagious, that kind of happiness.

Malini is shy, slim and small-boned like a bird, and speaks with quiet dignity, with Sujata translating for her.

'I'm 27,' she starts, in answer to my first question, 'and I've lived here with my daughter, who's eight, for two and a half years.'

'What was your life like, before coming here?'

'When I was young, I lost my mum. My dad had a second marriage but my aunts and uncles brought me up. I have ten brothers and sisters. I used to be in touch with them but after they knew my sickness, I didn't see them. I got married in 1994. It was an arranged marriage, to

Daljeet; I wasn't aware of his sickness. He wasn't HIV Positive when he got married but he was feeling sick often and his sister told him to get tested, but he didn't tell me.'

'When did you know about it?'

'I didn't find out till my husband died.'

I can't imagine the shock of that.

'How did you feel?'

She bursts into tears. I catch hold of her hand, ashamed of having caused her to lose her precarious composure.

I'm aware, being here, of many questions I have to leave unasked. Journalists learn not to avoid the obvious questions; the answers reveal details, the personal view, that the interviewee might not consider worth mentioning. But going for the details, in such fragile lives as these, can feel like going for the jugular. I had hoped not to do this.

Sujata waits, supportive but not intervening, till Malini recovers.

'I'm sorry,' I say.

'It's all right. It happens to me when I think of it.'

'Do you want to leave this?'

'No, I'll go on. The family didn't want the daughter-in-law once the son was dead,' Malini continues.

'This is common,' Sujata comments, when she translates this.

I don't want to ask Malini how she felt about that, but she answers the question without being asked.

'I didn't like it, being there: they started harassing me to find a job and support myself. I went to my gran's village but no one wanted me because of the sickness. When my child Jyoti was four, I found she also was HIV Positive. She had a very big stomach and malaria and wasn't eating.'

When Jyoti was taken to hospital Malini, as her mother, moved into the hospital too. 'When someone homeless gets admitted into hospital they stay there for months,' Malini explains, 'because they don't know anywhere to go. While my daughter was in hospital, I was seen by a social worker who put me in touch with Oasis. I was referred to Oasis in April 2003.'

'How did you feel about coming here, Malini?'

Her eyes light up suddenly. 'I am very happy! I studied up to Seventh Standard,' she explains, 'and I wanted to learn tailoring but I didn't have enough money to buy a machine, but when I came here I could do it. I made dresses, blouses, bags – everything!'

'How did Jyoti take to coming to live here?'

'Jyoti used to fall often,' Malini says, 'but she's now very well. Her health has improved since coming here.'

She thinks for a moment, then says, 'I have love here that I never got in my home.'

'How was it for you, coming into a home that was run by Christians? Did that bother you?'

'I'm from a Hindu family,' Malini explains. 'I had heard about Jesus and knew about the Christian religion but didn't believe anything. Here, I started listening to the times of worship and my faith has increased, little by little. On the TV channels, my sister-in-law saw something about Jesus and told me to say this prayer. I read the Bible and I pray now. I believe I can ask God for things.

'Jyoti goes for regular check-ups in hospital and the child in the next bed was on oxygen and the mother saw me praying and singing and asked, "Who do you worship?" I told her I worship Jesus and she asked me to pray for her child. So I prayed for the child and the next day the doctors said he was fine. They removed all the tubes and he was sent home.'

'How do you see your life here now?'

'I have a desire for my life to be a God-led plan,' Malini says. 'I'd like to be either a trainer or serve the Lord in whatever way he wants me to go.'

'Is there anything you would like to say to people who might read about you?'

'I want to highlight my story,' Malini says, 'so that people should know if they have faith in Jesus they win the kingdom of God. I want to give the gospel to as many people as possible.'

We go downstairs and find John, and Sujata invites us back to her flat to have a cold drink and relax.

A couple of little boys run in and tug at John's hand, so he tells Sujata, 'We'll follow you in a minute.'

One of the women points to the smaller child and tells John, 'It's his birthday.'

'That's terrific. How old are you now, Sudeep?'

'Five,' he says proudly.

'Happy birthday,' I say. He comes over and solemnly extends a hand to be shaken in congratulations and the woman laughs. 'He is full of life.'

'I can see that,' John says.

The boys scamper off to play and we go to Sujata's flat.

I'm interested to know what kind of people would leave successful careers in the city to take on other people's children as well as their own, and assume responsibility for a 'House of Wholeness' in this beautiful but isolated place. Prakash and Sujata and their two boys live in part of one of the houses. Although their kitchen/living room is entered by its own front door, it's not self-contained as another door from the room opens into a children's dormitory, and other women and children live in the same house, along with the gap-year girls and volunteers. There is not a great deal of privacy.

Prakash is just forty and Sujata 37. Their wedding photo
shows a good-looking, confident young professional
couple, well educated and motivated for success in the
world. This is a couple who could be 'having it all'.

'So what are you doing here?' I ask, when we are comfortably seated and Sujata has brought us all cool fruit
juice. Sujata and Prakash laugh and say, 'We wonder
sometimes!' Prakash begins, 'I used to read stories about
street children, and when I became a Christian I read
about people taking children from the streets and par-
enting them and the children would go on to become
something.

'As I became a believer and got closer to God, I felt
"This is how I'd like to spend my life." I used to work for
an international bank. I thought it was good because I
could earn a lot of money and do this work with children but God told me, "Not your resources but my
resources!" When I met Sujata at church, I found she had
a similar care for orphans. Then one of the girls in our
church married a worker from Oasis, when Purnata
Bhavan was being planned. We talked to him and he
told us to talk to the director of Oasis but I didn't
because I thought, "This is getting serious!"'

'Were you having second thoughts?' I ask Prakash.

'Not second thoughts – I was still having first
thoughts! But our pastor told him we were interested.
The pastor called at the bank for a chat – so this was serious! When I saw all the plans of the buildings it really
excited me. So we did more praying and talking to our
pastor. It took only a year. In 1998 I resigned from my job
and we joined Oasis with another couple, and came up
here. We were very clear by then. Sujata was seven
months pregnant. She was school counsellor at a school
for the deaf, but she had a social work qualification. So
this is more her kind of work than mine!

'We lived for three months in the local town while Purnata Bhavan was being built, and we got to know the local people and shopkeepers. Our son was seven months old by this time. There was just one house when we moved in here and the first boy came. We were two couples and one volunteer. Within fifteen days, we had two mothers, four children, and two single girls and within four years two houses were running. The village was a bit of a shock: more isolated than we thought. We realised how lonely you can get; we were city-dwellers. There were no rickshaws, no television, no mobile phones – we had to walk up to the highway to the telephone booth – and frequent power cuts and water problems.

'It was monsoon – four months of heavy rain; very damp. We washed our clothes and they didn't dry for two weeks. But the work was going on well and we had good support. We got one telephone line but the company expected us to pay a bribe because they saw big buildings and thought we were rich. But we invited the manager to come and see our work and after that he was very helpful and got us four more lines. In 2002 our second son was born, and we went to Bombay for two and a half years to work with the Ashadeep project for street children, and set up the home for boys who come off the street.'

Sujata joins in now. 'It was nice, the boys' home,' she says. 'It was a smaller home, maximum seven boys, like a real family set-up. Our own sons were happy there. In the city, they had other things to do and they miss that now we're back at Purnata Bhavan, and we miss our home church. When we were asked to come back here in a leadership capacity, we brought all the boys from the home with us.'

'We are developing contacts with new people now,' Prakash says, 'and we have learned to trust God more.

There have been times, dealing with someone's difficult emotions, when we didn't know if we were doing the right thing. In residential work it's not so much the physical work but the emotions.'

'Before, we were more part of a team,' Sujata says. 'Now, as managers, we are always giving, to staff and residents, and the replenishing isn't happening much and we feel weary sometimes. Often our children feel we are more for the project than for the family.'

Prakash says, 'There's more planning and thinking ahead and hitting targets: the role is growing.'

I am thinking this is similar to how John's role has grown, from being an outreach worker to street children to being someone who spends of a lot of time drafting plans, holding meetings and chasing funds to sustain the projects.

He may be thinking the same, because he intervenes here. 'Once an organisation reaches a certain size, it needs more funding and more structures. It has to have strong leadership, not just people knowing their own role and doing it.'

'We have to put systems in place and set targets,' Prakash says, 'and people don't always like it. We found that the women here were not getting jobs; they were given a training here but the hours were relaxed and also the women were cooking, cleaning, and enjoying themselves in a community. But the quality demanded in jobs is high; people were sympathetic to them but they also demand quality of work. So when we came back, training became like business: nine to five, not going for tea and then not coming back, and we got outside help with the cleaning. We are getting orders for the work now, and a small percentage goes to the women, which they will get when they go from here.'

There is noise outside, feet running up the stairs and the voices of children.

'The older children are home from school,' Prakash says. He pushes open the door to the other room and goes in to chat to them – two boys and five girls – and to see them settled to do their homework, sitting cross-legged on the floor.

Prakash and Sujata's elder son comes in and says hello, takes a drink from the fridge and goes into his own room.

'It must be difficult here, balancing the needs of the children with your own children's need for your attention?' I suggest.

Sujata nods. 'I feel torn between work and family life. We get days off so we take a break, but living on the job is difficult. We need more staff now. Volunteers are a real blessing.'

'Do you feel you're achieving what you set out to do?'

Prakash returns as Sujata answers: 'We do feel we are looking after the orphans and widows.'

John adds, 'Community living is very difficult; there have been many ups and downs. It takes a toll, living and working with the same people.'

'Do you think volunteers and visitors are deterred from coming by the HIV issue?'

'Yes,' Sujata says. 'We found people in our church stayed away from us because we were working with HIV. People still don't understand that it's not contagious. We held awareness programmes in the local school and invited parents, and we have invited people here to see for themselves, and that's helped. People expected the people here to be sick and dying.'

'Esther mentioned facing prejudice at school,' I say, 'from the parents and some of the teachers, as well as the children.'

'Arun was getting trouble at school,' Sujata agrees, 'and teachers weren't always helpful, and he's getting a lot of infections. So we are trying to give him more education at home now, the same syllabus and preparation for exams.'

I think of the little face looking over the banister when we first arrived, Arun's ease in following the women around while they were cooking and cleaning, his man-to-man stance while talking to John, and feel relieved. He seems at home here where he can be a small boy in a big family, unlike at school where he stands out and is seen as an AIDS victim.

I wonder, though, about Sujata – whether she is really at home here or if the life is too far removed from the city house-parent role she was comfortable with.

'Do you feel at home here?' I ask her, while Prakash returns to the children and John prepares to leave.

'I believe we're doing what we were called to do,' Sujata says. Then she says something that will stay with me, because it is in so much contrast to the life-improvement philosophies being marketed at home.

'Personally, my needs aren't met here,' she says, 'but I am fulfilled, because I know I am doing God's will.'

As we drive away from Purnata Bhavan, John stops by the signpost at the entrance to the driveway so I can take a photo of the place, looking back.

'Do the people living here mind about the sign?' I ask him. 'It kind of advertises the fact that they have HIV and AIDS.'

'No – people in the neighbourhood know anyway and it's best to be upfront about it. We're not hiding anything.'

'Do you worry about the risk to the children living here who don't have the virus, in case they pick it up from the other kids?'

We are leaving the gravel track and are back on the main road now, starting the descent towards the city.

'The risk isn't that great, and the children are taught to take certain precautions. It's probably more of a risk for the staff because they treat the kids. But it actually isn't that easy to catch.'

'It still seems to be a controversial issue.'

'It is. One of the most difficult decisions I had to make was whether to admit two children there who weren't HIV Positive, simply because they had nowhere else to go. We wouldn't normally take in children like that; we refer them to other agencies, like they refer children to us sometimes. But the Ashadeep team found two children living on the railway platform literally starving. When I saw the little boy I realised we didn't have time to do a referral because that can take up to four days and we didn't think he had that long to live.

'He was two years old but the size of a baby, emaciated and very weak. When he came to Purnata Bhavan, Prakash said he weighed the same as their 6-month old son.'

'Were the children orphans?'

'No, the parents had split up and were with other partners and left the children to fend for themselves – a two-year old boy with his five-year old sister as sole carer. They were both very dirty, thin and starving. I had to make a decision quickly, so I brought them here. It was a controversial decision and I got some stick for it, but I prayed and it seemed the right thing to do.'

'Where are they now?'

'Still there. Sreeja was one of the little girls in the dormitory, doing her homework, and Sudeep – you met Sudeep who is five today.'

'The birthday boy – the one who shook hands?'

'Yes.'

'You made the right decision, then.'

'I know that now but it was scary at the time.'

The air quality declines as we approach Mumbai. I wonder how Sujata can miss the crowds and the pollution but any city that appears to a visiting stranger as a solid mass of people is, to the people who live there, a network of smaller communities of people they know, live alongside and work with.

I think of the church service held in the dark old cinema and our church at home trying to raise funds and enthusiasm for a new building. If, as is often preached, the church is the people and not the building, then a city is the same thing – a living body of people, not a street plan or infrastructure. A city breathes. As we enter Mumbai, it seems to me that this city breathes with difficulty, like an asthmatic, ill at ease in its tight-to-bursting skin.

One question that many westerners ask about Indian poverty is, 'What caste are the poor people?' Yet the poorest of any nation are those with no caste, no standing in any social system. At one of the London churches I attend I meet the leader of an international organisation for Dalits, a few months after my return home. The Dalit people are classed as Untouchables – the lowest caste in the Hindu system. Yet, Raj tells me, they are not Hindus. 'Not originally. They are the original people of India. It's the Hindus who have made them a Hindu caste and said they are the lowest. Dalits are the third poorest social group globally, not just the poorest in India. They have no voice, no rights.'

The families in Bandra slum are from different backgrounds but all outcasts, outside the system in one way or another. Every nation has its caste system and its unclassified outcasts – the people who don't fit in or don't count, in the eyes of the powers-that-be or the 'wannabes'.

Another frequent question about India's poverty is, 'How many children do they have?' A couple of decades ago, the average was six to a family; today it is reckoned to be two. I am struck by sudden rage in a prayer meeting, when I return to the UK, when a church member comments casually that there may be something to be said for China's one-child policy and perhaps it could be applied in India. It's a temptation for human beings, faced with vast problems, to look for simple explanations and simple solutions. But human beings are not simple and it demeans all of us to do that.

The Indian children I have met have not been the cause of their parents' or their nation's suffering. They are individuals precious to God and to their communities. Many of them work to help support their parents, grandparents and younger siblings. Most are very far from taking life for granted or expecting the world to fulfil their wishes for them.

To regard them as a burden on the world is sickening. The world doesn't need fewer such children; it needs parents of affluent children to resist over-indulgence and teach them to care for the wider human family.

Charmaine is tired and so am I but the idea of going to cell group still appeals, so we change and get a rickshaw to 'Aunty's' house. The water supply has been shut off so there's no chance of a shower first. At Aunty's the ceiling fans are working and a window is open, but there seems to be no air. Everyone complains of the unseasonal heat.

This Aunty is one of the ladies who accommodates young Oasis girls from the UK in her home; there are two here this evening, along with the regular group members.

Included are prayers for one another's current needs. Charmaine asks for prayer for John's and my projected trip to Bangalore tomorrow and for the factors that might hinder it, particularly health issues. I had another attack of diarrhoea on returning home this evening – not good news when there's no water supply – and have swollen legs again and feel very tired.

The group prays seriously for God's blessing on the trip, for protection for me and for John, and Ramona who is leading the group this evening prays for my stay here: 'this labour of love'. I feel encouraged by the phrase. Swollen legs, nausea, tiredness and stomach cramps are, after all, normal precursors to labour.

Finally, Ramona suggests we take five minutes of silence to listen to anything the Lord might wish to say. 'He will speak to each one,' she emphasises. 'We must expect it.'

I fully agree with this. People talk about God, at God and to God a lot more than we listen and wait for him to answer. But if I'm honest, I don't expect to hear him in the thick noisy silence tonight. I'm too hot to think about anything except how much I need the next waft of warmish air from the ceiling fan or the rare wisp of breeze through the open window.

Towards the end of the time, though, I hear: 'You can't cope with the heat – but when the breeze comes, you can. And you can't cope with the circumstances – but when my Spirit comes, you can.'

'Lord,' I prayed, 'I can't possibly go to Bangalore, or anywhere, as I am. If you want me to go, you'll have to get me there.'

Clearly then, I hear him. 'I will raise you up on eagle's wings.'

That's all right, then. I'm going.

Chapter 15

On Eagle's Wings

I never thought about eagle flight. It looks from the ground like a smooth and exhilarating glide but when you're the eaglet riding pillion on parent wings you can get pretty airsick from all those balletic swoops.

Having gone back to John and Charmaine's after the prayer meeting feeling peaceful and confident, I spend most of the night in the bathroom.

The water supply is back on so at least I can flush the loo, though I'm afraid of waking everyone by flushing it so often.

I have another dialogue with God in the night, about the practicalities of taking another plane journey while still having swollen legs from the last flight, and the impossibility of visiting the toilet every twenty minutes on a five hundred mile journey. The answer isn't so clear this time but I think I hear, either from God or from my guts, 'You need to get out of Bombay.'

In the morning, Charmaine says, 'You'd better not go,' and John says, 'You're not well,' both of which sound practical. I tell them about the 'eagle's wings' message of last night and say I think I should go, and they accept it. After the children have left for school, we sit down and pray for the trip, and for Charmaine left at home with sole responsibility for the children – something she has to face quite often, with John's frequent travels around the three cities where Oasis leads or shares projects.

We go into the office for a while before leaving to catch the flight. The office staff complain good-naturedly that John periodically introduces a new office assistant who needs intensive instruction, then as soon as he becomes useful promotes him and brings in another untrained street boy.

The current office assistant is Rushil. Very new to the job and looking very young in his immaculate shirt, trousers and clean shoes, he is alert to the staff's calls to fetch files, make coffee or learn new computer skills.

I sit and look through the book of photos of Oasis' people till John finishes work in his office and Leena sends out for early lunch for us both. Rushil sets out a small table carefully, attentive to detail. I ask him how long he has been office assistant for Oasis and he says, 'One month only.'

'Do you like the job, Rushil?'

His eyes light up and he smiles. 'I *like* the job!'

'What do you like about it?'

'They trust me.'

As at Purnata Bhavan yesterday, I suddenly feel like crying. Rushil finishes laying the table and moves away. I can't get upset now, while I'm here and need to focus on listening and transcribing people's stories. Their lives don't sound exceptional to them; they are matter-of-fact about details which strike me as tragic, poignant, admirable or plain miraculous. The best I can do is try to convey an accurate account of what the people I meet here say and how they live life in the conditions they have chosen or have been given. Time enough to indulge in unproductive emotion when I get home.

Or so I think. As it turns out, I have forgotten to consult God about this pragmatic – or cowardly – postponement of inconvenient feelings, and he has other ideas, as I will discover in Bangalore. Flying to Bangalore is the easy way. John used to do the trip by train, which takes 24 hours. Now that he travels there once a month or more, and to Chennai (Madras) in the east, as well as occasional meetings in the UK, that isn't feasible. He has also done the Bangalore trip by motorbike but wouldn't want to repeat it nowadays.

Arriving at Bangalore airport, we're accosted by rickshaw drivers but John bypasses them. 'Aren't we getting a rickshaw to the office?' I ask.

'Yes but not these. They rip you off. There's a pre-pay system here.'

We join a queue at an outdoor desk where a man issues tickets for rickshaws. Our driver wears a handkerchief over his mouth. I guess the pollution must be as bad here as in Mumbai but the roads seem less crowded and the pace of traffic less frenetic. Downtown Bangalore also seems a lot more westernised, with a number of familiar chain store names.

A curious incident takes place on the way to the office. We've stopped at traffic lights when a young boy comes by selling boxes of tissues.

'No thanks,' John says. He waits for the boy to move on to the next vehicle in the queue but the boy stays.

'Only five rupees.'

'No thanks.'

'Four.'

'No – no tissues at any price, thank you!'

'Three rupees.'

'No.'

'OK sir, two box. Two box for three rupees.'

'No! Thank you.'

'Three box for three rupees.'

The rickshaw driver turns round and chortles, holding his hand over his handkerchiefed mouth.

'Look, try the next car!' John says. 'I don't want tissues, all right?'

The boy's face contorts. He goes to move on, then stops.

'Four box for three rupees.'

I get the feeling he doesn't know why he's persisting. It's hardly worth his while selling them at this price; he might as well give them away.

'I am not sick!' John says, thumping his chest dramatically. 'I have no cold or cough, all right?'

The boy waves his head from side to side, but continues to stand there. An odd thought goes through my mind: maybe he's a prophet. I dismiss it instantly. Maybe the sun is affecting my mental stability.

'Five box for three rupees,' says the boy, forlorn and embarrassed. Five boxes are all he has. I feel sorry for him and am tempted to buy them, but who needs five boxes of tissues? Or even one, on the way to the office? I've deliberately travelled light, being here for only one night.

The lights change and the rickshaw moves forward, leaving the boy standing there with his five boxes of tissues. I will remember him later on.

We go down a shady side street where construction work is in progress, the upper storey of a half-completed building supported by dozens of slim tree trunks and branches while the walls are being built up. Cows browse around the piles of rubble outside. The rickshaw driver swerves to avoid them and they meander into the road, dreamily aware of their invulnerability.

The Oasis office in Bangalore is in a residential street and looks like a house, with a balcony on the upper floor. We go upstairs through a workroom where women sit at sewing machines, with a small office beyond it accommodating three people – one of them

Brenda, the English woman I met briefly at the training centre on my first day in Mumbai. Up more stairs there is a computer training room, then a large pattern cutting, sewing and packing workshop where some women sit at sewing machines, trainees sit on the floor studying diagrams, and an unsmiling man stands at a table cutting fabric, preoccupied with his work. A desk with a computer workstation is tucked into a corner of the landing beside a cabinet, and the main office is beyond it, with a toilet accessed through the office. As in other Oasis premises, multiple uses are made of every available space and the office is full of chairs and desks.

I meet Anita, director of the projects in Bangalore, who is heavily pregnant; Vasu, a man I've already heard mentioned by Rahul, who now oversees all the health care; and Majella, the administrator, a lively and smiling lady who starts teasing John the moment he walks in and who shortly suggests sending out for his favourite Bangalore speciality snacks.

We sit and chat and eat, though nausea prevents me from doing much of the latter. Brenda comes in to say hello again. A former textiles teacher, she works here overseeing the design and production of bags, clothes, accessories and home furnishings for sale in local boutiques and for export, and supervising the training in sewing and textiles.

'I'll see you later,' she promises, as the office empties and I sit down with Anita to hear about what goes on in Bangalore. 'Maybe we can all go for a meal when you finish here for the day.' A meal doesn't sound appealing but I'd be interested to hear from her what brings a middle-aged English woman to work in Bangalore.

Anita explains that Oasis in Bangalore is a training centre, workshop and production company. East West Education, a UK charity, pays the rent, training and girls' salaries and Oasis gives the girls a travel allowance. 'We're covering our costs but not making a profit, though we could in the future,' Anita says. She gives details of the day care centre for pre-school children, the slum projects, the Back To School programme for drop-outs, and the training in literacy, numeracy, IT, health care, tailoring and English. It's impressive.

'The women in the slum communities want to start small businesses making poppadoms, jams, pickles and *dosa* batter, packaging and selling it. We're planning to do some training for that, set hygiene standards, and market the products through churches and local contacts.'

Anita goes on to talk about the anti-trafficking campaign that is one of Oasis' current priorities. Tomorrow's meeting – John's reason for being here – will bring together Oasis directors from Mumbai, Chennai and Bangalore to discuss progress and future plans.

'The Missing Persons' Bureau set up by the Bangalore Police Commissioner's Office is the first in India,' Anita explains. 'Oasis designed computer software for police stations to share information when someone goes missing. There are eighty-eight police stations in Bangalore alone. In the first seven months of using the new system, there were 1,400 cases, and the police have been able to close some cases which were open for the last five years.'

'We're talking about women being trafficked for prostitution?' I ask.

'Yes, there are the pimps, and also some children and young women get kidnapped by beggars. And there are traffickers for labour.'

'Is human trafficking as widespread in Bangalore as in Mumbai?'

'The state of Karnataka is second only to Maharashtra in terms of trafficking. Bangalore is a transit zone. We're trying to get some figures but it's hard to tell whether someone is a runaway, has got lost or been trafficked. Oasis is increasingly involved with anti-trafficking work. We're working with the government homes; trafficked children and young women who are picked up by the police are compulsorily taken there and kept for four months maximum but sometimes they're not traced or there's no one to take them back. Some children are never claimed. We hope to help repatriate the ones who want to go home, and follow them up to make sure the home is suitable and they don't get re-trafficked.'

I think of the women I've talked to – Sanam sold by her own aunt, Haneefa by her friend's husband, and Esha and Sharmila by 'kind ladies' – and realise this concern is justified: a home that welcomes a son or daughter back could sell them or place them at risk of being abducted again.

'We also want to provide psycho-social care and health care,' Anita says, 'as well as refurbishing the children's homes; there are hardly any toys there – nothing.'

'What happens if children aren't claimed when the four month period is up?' I ask.

'They're put into long-term homes, some of them run by other organisations if the government ones are full. We want to make sure the children get continuity of education too, when they're moved to other homes.'

The plans for helping trafficked children sound ambitious, on top of all Oasis' existing projects in Bangalore.

'How many staff do you have here?' I ask Anita.

'A total of twenty in Bangalore. On the trafficking project, just me, and staff to be appointed. Majella, who is currently doing admin work, will be doing counselling two days a week. The majority of the staff are working in the community, with some volunteers from local churches. Students who drop out of school have a chance to go to school at the church, Monday to Friday, and come to Oasis once a week. We're part of the National Open School system. Some of the staff come back in the evenings to help.

'Since 2002 there's been a boom in jobs in Bangalore – it's the call-centre capital now. That's led to more jobs for lower class families too, in the homes of the workers, so it's helped everybody. You'll go into the slum community tomorrow and meet some of the people working there, and there's a picnic for the slum children in the morning.'

I ask whether the slum has a language problem like the Bandra one, or if the people there are local.

'They're mostly migrants. Kannada is the local language spoken here. Tamil is also common because Tamil Nadu is the next state and a lot of people in the slum are from there, or from Andhra Pradesh.'

'How have they reacted to you as a Christian organisation?'

'We had a lot of opposition by the local government co-operator in charge of the area, who is in the BJP party – very anti-Christian. He's a local *goonda*, beats people up, and he threatened to break up our office and throw us out. We said, "We're doing social work, not converting people, and the fact that we are Christians doesn't mean you should threaten us." We spoke to the MP, because this man is only a member of the local legislative assembly, supposedly answerable to him, but the MP said, "You can register a complaint with the police but we don't want to make an issue of it and start a history." So we just prayed a lot about it, and it died down completely.'

'Is it forbidden to do anything that might lead to people converting, here?'

'Schools do say prayers with children, depending on which background they are from, and our crèche and *balwadi* children say a prayer. If someone in the community is in a crisis or has a problem, we offer to pray, but generally we try to leave the prayer side to the local church so we keep to social work and don't get seen as a church.'

'Do all the Oasis workers have to be Christian, including those who come from the community?' I ask Anita.

'All of our staff are committed believers – not just Christian because they were christened,' she says. 'All our projects started with prayer and if there's a problem our first move is always to pray. People do actually look to us for that now; whatever their background, they accept that we are totally dependent on God – that he works through us; it's not us. Every Friday the staff meet to pray; we sometimes go on retreats, and staff have said they'd like to have a prayer partner within the staff – to be accountable in their work and prayer life to someone outside their church and family.'

Anita sits back. I ask how soon her baby is due and she smiles and says, 'Two weeks!'

'Do you have other children?'

'One little girl. She'll come in here soon.'

'Do you find it stressful trying to balance the demands of work and family, especially so close to the new baby coming?'

She smiles wryly and says, 'I'm used to the work here. I joined Oasis in 1999 but took a break of two years when my first child was born and came back in 2004 – though Oasis has stretchable arms: I took emergency calls while I was away, if kids weren't well and decisions had to be made. The two years out were a time to reflect, and coming back was such a sense of peace and belonging and being in the right place doing the right thing.'

I think of Sujata at Purnata Bhavan saying, 'My needs are not met here but I am fulfilled,' and ask Anita, 'Are your needs being met, in this work?'

'No, I'm still struggling with tiredness, time and work. All of us have commitments to work and family – but I don't struggle with not being at peace. And I think all the staff would say that as well, and all the people who have made commitments to Christ in their work. They find a tremendous sense of fulfilment and satisfaction.'

Anita stretches and yawns, laughing at herself. She looks tired and says, 'Yes, I'm coming,' as her little daughter runs in and asks, 'Are we going home soon?'

But she gets delayed by someone asking for information, and I go out on to the balcony for some fresh air while she deals with the query. The little girl comes out too and we look out on the quiet street and the house opposite, where a toddler is taking shaky steps in the dusty front garden.

The cantor from a mosque nearby sings the call to prayer through a loudspeaker and the sun takes on a hazy effect.

I wave at the toddler and Anita's little girl waves too.

'Do you have a garden at home?' I ask her.

'Yes, I have. And I'm going to have a baby soon.'

'Are you excited?'

'Yes, I am. Where have you come from?'

'From England.'

She nods, satisfied. 'I knew.'

Only two more days in India. I wonder if England will seem different, when I go home. I feel I have been far away, in distance, time and experience.

'I hope you don't mind me saying, but you look so tired.' Brenda says, coming to find me. 'What happened?'

'Delhi belly – in Bombay!'

'Oh, are you OK to go out and eat this evening?'

'Yes, but I probably won't eat much. Do you live here permanently now?'

Brenda laughs. 'I came out here on a temporary basis, went back to my teaching job in England for two years but couldn't settle, so I came back here for another "temporary" job.'

John joins us and we walk towards the main road with its choice of small restaurants. I realise I've never asked John when his own residency in India ceased to be 'temporary'.

'When did you know you weren't going back home – that Oasis India was where you were meant to be now?' I ask him.

'Well, Oasis India didn't exist when I first came out; we were just building contacts with local churches. I don't know when I finally realised I was staying. When I married Charmaine, I suppose.'

Brenda stops in the street and faces me. 'I don't think going out for a meal is what you need,' she says. 'You should rest and eat something plain, like bananas and bread. Why don't we just go to my flat? Unless you're really hungry, John?'

'I'm not – the staff have been feeding me snacks all afternoon!'

So we head towards Brenda's flat, which is cool and spacious. She brings out trays of bread, crackers, salad, fruit and cool drinks, and we sit and chat for a while till her son phones from England. John says he'd be glad of an early night, so we say goodbye and take a rickshaw. I realise I don't know where we're staying the night; he had asked Majella to book rooms in one or another hostel.

'It's a theological college,' he says, when I ask. 'I've stayed there before; it's filled with prayer.'

There are big iron gates at the entrance, and a large notice just inside: DO NOT WALK ON THE LAWNS. After Brenda's easy hospitality, the contrast of this

welcome strikes me. A few steps further on another
notice shouts: DO NOT PLUCK THE FLOWERS. The
flowers all stand to attention and there are no gaps, so I
assume no one's had the temerity to pluck them. There's
an amazing tree with a shock of bright purple flowers
and no leaves, like a parrot in the wilderness. Before the
entrance doors, the driveway widens out into a perfect
circle of tarmac. An even larger notice here says: NO
PARKING IN THIS AREA.

The reception area is empty apart from two
American men who say hello briefly then return to
their conversation. We wait for a while then John asks
them if there is anyone around and they point down a
corridor. Eventually we find a man who says it is not
his responsibility and he is not expecting any guests
this evening.

'My office booked two rooms,' John explains, but the
man doesn't look impressed. 'Who should we speak to?'

The man goes off rather reluctantly to fetch someone
and we hear a conversation going on between him and
another man. While waiting, I read the notices in the
reception area. One says: WE <u>WARN</u> AGAINST WAST-
ING WATER (FILL ONE BUCKET OF COLD WATER
BEFORE COLLECTING HOT). I'm not sure how that
works but am unlikely to want hot water in this climate.

A further one says: DO NOT PASTE ANYTHING ON
WALLS.

Yet another one, which also merits underlining, states:
DO <u>NOT</u> ASK FOR REFUND IF YOU DO NOT EAT
BREAKFAST. I wonder if breakfast is so unpalatable that
many people have asked for refunds. The notices themselves would cause indigestion.

An older man in a suit appears. He states that no
booking has been received in writing and therefore no
rooms have been reserved.

There are a lot of rooms here, and the place is echoing with emptiness. John enquires politely whether there are vacant rooms available. The man goes into Hindi. John follows him. The man goes back into English. The problem appears to be that Majella has booked by phone and has, as the college insists, followed it up with a written letter but the letter has either not been received or has been mislaid. After a lot of discussion, the man agrees to let us have rooms. He moves into official welcoming mode, goes behind the counter, produces a book for us to sign and hands over keys.

I catch sight of another notice on the counter. Rather incongruously it says: MAY PEACE PREVAIL ON EARTH. I'm severely tempted to add in brackets: (BUT ONLY FOR THOSE WHO DON'T WALK ON OUR GRASS, PLUCK OUR FLOWERS, PARK IN OUR DRIVE, WASTE OUR WATER, DEFACE OUR WALLS, DEMAND COMPENSATION FOR OUR BREAK-FASTS *OR* FAIL TO RESERVE OUR ROOMS IN WRIT-ING).

I'm about to draw John's attention to the signs but he looks so tired I think better of it. I've seen enough of the way he works in this past week to realise that if he admits to being tired he's exhausted.

The rooms are clean, with bathrooms, and the ceiling fans work. John says goodnight and goes into his room. I spend a long time in the bathroom. The day's respite from diarrhoea has been temporary. As soon as I come back to the bedroom and prepare to go to bed, I have to go back to the loo. This is inconvenient, but not the worst. I then find I have a totally unscheduled period as well.

It can't be.

I have travelled light to Bangalore. I have nothing of any use with me. The thought flashes into my mind,

Why didn't I listen to the prophet at the crossroads? Five boxes of tissues would be really handy right now!

What am I going to do? I run through the options. I am five hundred miles from any women I know in the whole of India, apart from Brenda, whose phone number I don't have. I don't want to wake up John, who is exhausted and will probably be fast asleep by now. I really don't want to enquire of the unwelcoming manager whether this place keeps emergency supplies of the female variety. I have not seen any women staying here. I can't go out, in my present state, and wander up and down the road in the hope of finding a shop.

Having come to the end of my options, I look out into the corridor to see if there's anyone who might help. The two Americans and two staff are having a serious discussion together in the corridor about somebody's writings. I could walk up to them and ask . . . No, I couldn't.

The bathroom contains a rationed amount of loo paper and I have a few tissues. Shall I risk it? Wait till morning and hope for the best? I don't think so. I don't want to be the inspiration behind the creation of a new notice saying DO NOT BLEED ON OUR SHEETS. I hate to do this but I can't see any alternative. The only human being I've seen in this place is my nephew. I knock on his door. To my relief, he answers, and I explain the predicament.

So, Lord, was fear of embarrassment on your list of things you're healing me of, on this trip? If so, can we tick that one off now too?

John is instantly sympathetic. Not to worry, he says; there will still be shops open and he will go out and find a rickshaw. He's back within half an hour. I tell him he's a hero and he goes back to his room.

Crisis averted. I get into bed, pick up the book of psalms I've brought with me and read, *How lovely is your*

*dwelling place, Lord God of hosts! . . . They are happy who
dwell in your house, forever singing your praise. They are
happy whose strength is in you, in whose hearts are the roads
to Sion.*

It's true. Why do I worry? When am I going to learn
to trust God more? For every problem that comes, he has
a solution. Maybe not one I would have chosen or one
that's convenient, but he won't leave me helpless, even
in a frosty theological college in Bangalore.

I settle down and go to sleep, feeling happy and
singing God's praises. At 6 a.m. I am woken by violent
pains and find I am haemorrhaging. My faith flies out of
the window.

*Oh God, why is this happening? How could you do this to
me?*

I rush for the bathroom and the packet of bulky pads.
These are not going to last me long. I can't – *and won't, do
you hear me, God? –* wake John up again. Anyway, even
Indian shops are closed at this time of the morning. I
know I am panicking. Where is my faith? God doesn't
change. I am still 'dwelling in his house'. *And bleeding to
death alone in Bangalore!*

I fetch the book of psalms.

Lord, I pray, *I need to understand why this is happening.
You promised me your protection. Tell me what's going on?*

The lines of a psalm jump off the page at me.

*Against you alone, Lord, have I sinned. What is evil in your
sight, I have done.*

Jesus, what have I done? The phrase that resounds is,
in your sight. What is evil *in your sight* I have done. So it
may not be something that's evil in my sight, necessar-
ily? Nor in anyone else's. I'd know if I'd done something
recognisably evil. I have an uncomfortably nit-picky
conscience, usually.

Give me a clue, Lord.

The word that comes to mind then is *professional*. The penny drops. I have been keeping a professional distance from people, regarding them as interviewees. I have been trying to do a professional job, telling myself that what matters for now is to gather material to write case histories for Oasis, and maybe eventually a book. I haven't allowed myself to get too affected by these terribly painful life histories people keep telling me. Far more sensible, I've decided, to focus on getting the details right and the shorthand accurate and avoid ending up in an emotional heap. But what I've been doing, actually, is copping out. Protecting myself. Telling myself I can then go back to England, write something to enhance awareness of the needs of our brothers and sisters here, and ask my friends and my church to pray. Maybe use the written word to encourage donations to the worthwhile projects.

Except . . . none of that is what Jesus did, is it? What he did was bleed for us. I see, suddenly, that I have not been letting myself bleed. Unsurprising, then, that my body is now doing it for me. It's not my problem, after all, if I become an emotional heap, as long as I'm an emotional heap at the foot of the cross. I don't like this way of doing things. I argue with God while sitting on the loo at 6-something in the morning.

Listen, Lord, there are all these people at home – and some in India now too – who are praying for me to be in good health on this trip, yet it's been one thing after another: swollen legs, diarrhoea, now this. This whole trip would have been far easier if I'd just left the body at home and come without it!

Swiftly, I hear the answer – loud and clear: *Is that what I did?*

I have a sudden image of Jesus' body, hanging on the cross. In agony.

I feel really, really ashamed.

Jesus, I pray, OK, I'll do it your way. I know I'm too super-ficial, and I haven't experienced enough of what these people have been through, to be capable of feeling a fraction of what they feel. But let me feel that fraction now.

Phrases and faces come into my mind, lucidly and inescapably.

Esther from Purnata Bhavan, having lost both parents, talking about her little brother Arun with HIV: *'I feel very scared from inside.'*

Sharmila from the brothel: *'I don't want to do this dirty work!'*

Pranad, living on the railway platform at 12 years old: *'We had to pick up dead bodies on the line.'*

Madhukshi at Purnata Bhavan, having lost her baby and her husband to AIDS: *'And then my daughter died.'*

Smita saying of Sanam, *'At the age of 7 her aunty sold her.'*

It hits me then. A tiny fraction of what God feels. But it is agony.

Chapter 16

Finding Angels

Angels come in many shapes and forms. Majella comes in a gold-coloured *shalwar kameez* with black *dupatta*, a wide smile, loud laugh and exuberant personality. The halo is invisible. In response to a discreet briefing from John, she whisks me out of the office building as soon as we arrive there in the morning and takes me to the pharmacy nearby.

Soul and body both calmed down after the onslaught of grief early in the morning and I sat up in bed alternately praying and dozing till non-refundable breakfast time, which turned out to be nothing more threatening than cornflakes with hot milk or *dosas* with watery filling.

I will not be able to run about with the slum children on their picnic this morning for three hours, nor visit the women in the slum in the afternoon, where toilets are not easily accessible. But I can do interviews if people come to the office, as John suggests.

Hence Majella. On the way to the pharmacy, she hugs my arm and says, 'I know what it's like; it makes you so tired! What do you want me to ask the pharmacist for, for you?' she asks.

'What's Hindi for super-ultra-mega-absorbency?'

She laughs and says, 'We don't speak Hindi here. The language of Karnataka province is Kannada.'

On the way back, she points out a snack bar. 'It's not open yet but later I'll come back and buy you fruit juice; they make it fresh and it will give you some energy. And for lunch I'll get you some buns. A lot of visitors here get upset stomach.'

The meeting on human trafficking will take up most of the day. Slavery is a hidden evil, protected by many people's belief it could never happen in their nation or territory – but it's global, and it does.

The toilet is en suite to the office, where the meeting is going on.

'Just walk in and out,' John says. 'No one will take any notice.'

Majella goes to call Roshni, a former trainee from the slum community who is now an Oasis employee. I feel less enthusiasm today for meeting more people and hearing more stories, perhaps because my physical state renders me slow-thinking or perhaps because I feel it will be more of the same as I've heard before. By the end of the day I'm not only ashamed of my cynicism but appalled at the thought that I could have missed out on meeting these people. It strikes me, being here, that the life of every person is valid and unique and that their inner victories may never be known to anyone except God, to whom they are extremely precious.

Roshni is a local 21-year-old girl who lives in the slum community and first came to Oasis as a tailoring trainee. Now she's a trainer and supervisor in Oasis's production company, Jacob's Well.

Majella installs us all at the desk on the landing, whose occupant is away today.

The starting point of Roshni's story is: 'I come from a Hindu background but my mother and father and my sister and I accepted Jesus. Near my house we have a church and Oasis came there. My dad had heart trouble and was in hospital and they came to see him and told him about God, but my dad was an alcoholic and he wouldn't listen to them. Then the doctor told my dad that within one day he will die, and the church had a watch-night prayer and we prayed for him all night and he was well, and he believed God touched him.

'At fourteen, I was going to school and working – doing housework – as well, and so I discontinued my studies in Eighth Standard.'

Majella intervenes here. 'A lot of girls are taken out of school by their parents when they reach puberty.'

'Oh – leaving school wasn't your choice, Roshni?'

I think of friends' children at home begging their parents to let them leave school as soon as they can and the parents trying to persuade them to persevere with their education.

'My mum and dad made a marriage for me when I was fourteen,' Roshni explained.

'You got married at fourteen? That's very young! Did you know him, before you got married?'

'I didn't know the man,' Roshni says. 'He was a neighbour to us but I didn't see him or talk to him before.' Seeing the expression on my face, she laughs and says, 'That's the culture.'

'Did you leave home and go and live with him straight away?'

'Yes, but it's not far away. My husband is from the village, not from Bangalore, but my mum told him, "You stay in Bangalore, near me."'

'Did you find it hard to adjust to married life, at fourteen?'

Roshni giggles. 'I was not mature in my mind and I was always fighting with my husband!'

On the other hand, maybe Western parents might quite like the idea of marrying off their feisty fourteen-year old daughters and letting someone else deal with the adolescent rebellions. Roshni doesn't quite fit the image of the demure young wife submitting meekly to an arranged marriage, dominated by a stranger of a husband.

'Do you still fight?'

'I am more mature now,' she says seriously, 'and he has accepted Jesus so it is easier. My mum said she wouldn't marry me to a Hindu so he said he will convert, and now he believes in his heart.

'When I came to Oasis as a trainee I was just married. Then I had my daughter, who is five now. We had a difficulty with the training because I couldn't earn money but we prayed and we managed on what my husband earned. There was a two-year contract with Levi, and for the work we had a good training in tailoring. Then for one year I was at home and for one year I went to ITC – a big company – and worked in the factory. They had computerised sewing machines! Then I got pregnant again and the doctor said, "Don't work," and my husband told me not to.

'Oasis started a production unit here and I came and asked if I could teach the trainees, but I didn't think they would give me the job of supervisor. I was happy that they give me this job. They trust me, and Brenda gave me training in how to teach the girls, and I must thank God he gave me nice people. I did one year as teacher, then I took more training in English, and now I do the shopping and accounts and marketing. I call people to come in at Christmas time, or I call the shops and take the orders when Brenda isn't there, and send the products to the UK and overseas. In the beginning I was afraid to do all these things and at first Brenda came with me, but now I do it. And my second daughter is five months old now.'

'How many girls at a time do you take for training?'

'We had eight girls training here last year but only five took the certificate because some got married. We take a maximum of ten trainees at one time. In the training period we are told about Jesus, as well as doing English classes and computers.'

'Have you changed, since being here?'

It's a question I've asked a lot of the people. I'm interested to know what makes people change, deep down.

Roshni nods emphatically. 'I started to trust the Lord in small things and he has brought me up; I believe very much. I am from a very poor background in the slums. It was too difficult to live there – no work, and my father a drunkard and my mother going out to do housework; she had to find dowries for marriage. It's too difficult to study in that area. Even now, my father beats my mother and drinks; we are praying for him. After the hospital, he was OK for two years and he came to church, but after that he didn't come.'

'Are you still living in the slum now?'

'Yes, I am still there. For us it's going well, with money for looking after the children as they're growing. My husband works as a driver. But we don't have facilities or water. In the rains, it's not too bad in our slums; the flood doesn't come in the houses, but in some areas they have that. Also there are problems with neighbours: they come and fight, using bad language, and the children don't grow up well. After I came here I could see how the people in the slum are. The parents leave the children outside; they earn for themselves and eat and drink. They don't buy food or clothes or anything for the children, or think about their future. The children go hungry and aren't cared for; they have to beg.'

'Are you planning to leave the slum, then, if you can afford to live somewhere else?'

I'm surprised when Roshni shakes her head emphatically.

'It's a good witness to Christ to live in the slum and live differently,' she says. 'People come to my door to fight and I don't join in, and when I listen to what they say and don't fight with them, they go silent and go away and don't give more trouble.'

Wow.

'Is there anything else you'd like to say, Roshni?'

She smiles. 'Come and see our work.' She takes me into the workroom and shows me the different processes being engaged in by groups of women and girls, and opens cupboards to show me the products, neatly stacked: cushion covers and bags and clothes and other items. They're attractive, some traditional Indian designs and some contemporary.

'Can I come back later and buy a few things for presents?'

'What do you like?'

'Maybe a couple of bags and some cushion covers.'

'We'll have them ready for you to look. You can see them properly, in the light.'

In this light, I can see Roshni as a supervisor now, no longer a slum girl but a confident and productive member of her company.

Tiptoeing through the meeting again to the loo, it occurs to me that Oasis doesn't approach a project by considering realistically what it can do as a small organisation, but starts with the need. In the case of human trafficking, the need is huge – overwhelming. What can one small group of people do? But then, fifteen years ago the charity wasn't even one small group, just three individuals looking for a way to do something for people with no one to speak for them.

Within a few months of today's meeting, John's newsletter will confirm that Oasis has small teams visiting the homes for rescued children, counselling and providing health care. New staff have been taken on and trained and the work has started. Plans don't stay long in the planning stage here, before being translated into action.

Majella has gone out on visits in the slum community. I sit at the desk at the top of the stairs and read through some of my notes. Snippets of last night's conversation at Brenda's flat come back to me. I don't really understand what prompted a woman in her fifties, who had hardly even been abroad, to leave four children at home – albeit almost grown-up ones – and come to Bangalore. She seems a quiet person, not the type to go round the world for a mid-life adventure. I go down to the office Brenda shares with two IT tutors to ask whether she would have time to tell me more.

'You look awful,' she greets me.

'Thanks a lot!' I tell her what happened in the night.

'Why didn't you phone me? I wish I'd asked you to stay now! Do you want to go back to my flat and rest for the day?'

'I don't feel too bad, thanks. I was wondering if you'd be willing to be an interviewee?'

She laughs. 'No one would be interested in me!'

'How many Englishwomen of our age do you know who do what you're doing?'

'Well . . . OK then! What do you want to know?'

'How did you come to be here, for a start?'

'I became a Christian at twenty,' Brenda begins, 'and at the same time felt that I would go to Nepal. It didn't make any sense to me; I didn't know that the place existed or where it was! I finished my degree and taught textiles and art in a new comprehensive for a year. I didn't do anything about finding out about Nepal. At university I'd been part of a very vibrant group of Christians, and two were working for Manchester City Mission and at their invitation I went to do vocational training with women on a very rough estate.

'Since then I've had a passion for helping women who don't have opportunities, as well as a passion for my skills – tailoring and design. I did too much and got exhausted, and decided to move near a friend and take a teaching job.

'At church, they introduced me to another teacher who was looking for someone to share a house and she had just come from Nepal! I shared a house with her for a year and prayed a lot with her. Nepal sounded wonderful; she said the people were gentle, and the textiles were amazing.

'I met my husband, got married and had four children. When my eldest son was thirteen, he persuaded my friend to do Radio Cracker and Crackerteria, a Christmas project set up by Steve Chalke to make people aware and raise funds for India. Then six years ago, I'd had a divorce and was teaching full-time in a church school. I loved the job. But this stirring in my heart came again, to share my skills with women in Asia where tailoring gives women real opportunities. My daughter had been out to Peru for a gap year with Oasis and brought me a leaflet about Jacob's Well in Mumbai. She suggested that I found out more about it. At school, the Head didn't mind me taking a sabbatical for six months.

'I talked with the vicar as well – I'm Church of England – because I felt I should be with my kids, who were 16, 18, 20 and 23 then. I thought I'd wait till the youngest one was at university. But the vicar said, "With God, it's not always convenient! A friend of mine told God he couldn't go now because his children were young, then his mother wasn't well, then he finally applied for ministry and got turned down because he was too old." My kids were very positive about it. They stayed with my best friend next door, and my mum was not far away.'

'What about Nepal?' I ask.

'Nepal was still in my mind. When I went for my interview, Oasis weren't working in Nepal, but what I wanted was to go from October to March, to work with women and to use my tailoring skills, and the man who interviewed me said, "It just so happens that Bangalore needs a trainer for six months, for women. They're three months into a nine-month training for a contract with Levi Strauss but the person in charge has too much to do."'

'And you hadn't been to India before?'

'I'd never been anywhere further than France and Spain! I raised the money to go for six months, from savings and from my church, and I left. When I came here I loved it, the colour, the textiles, and the vitality and warmth of the Indian people. I achieved the training and also placed the girls: they were given jobs with Levi's. But the journey was two buses, it was longer working hours and I wasn't there to encourage them and they dropped out. I went back to the UK and on the plane God said he wanted me to make plans to come back. My son had two more years at school so I planned to come back in two years, with a view to going for longer – and connecting in some way with Nepal.

'I came back to Bangalore but it was different management and it was a little bit difficult. I knew in my heart that God wanted me here, and my contract was for two years, but it wasn't easy: I'm a person who questions things and I wasn't very popular, especially as a foreigner. It became easier, but in the first days I questioned God: "I could be at home with my family; what am I doing here?"'

John later fills in details, saying the previous manager didn't treat the staff as team members and Brenda had been courageous in speaking up for them all and had a hard time for a while, before changes were made in the management.

'After two years, before going back to the UK, I took three days off to pray and fast. I felt God saying to me, "I haven't called you for two years; I've called you for life." '

'How did you feel about that?' I ask.

'I couldn't see how it could happen. When I got home my mother, who's eighty, said, "That's enough now; you aren't going back."'

'How did your children react?'

'Very differently. My eldest son said, "You've got four kids and you need to get the family together again, and you won't have any pension." My youngest son said, "You just do your own thing; it's up to you, Mum!" My younger daughter said she'd prefer it if I was in the UK, and my elder daughter said, "You can always come home if it doesn't work out!" And people in the church said it was wonderful, what I was doing, but didn't I mean to go to Nepal? I was totally confused! Now I'm on another two-year contract but I feel in my heart I will go to Nepal. But John says, "Don't even think about it!"'

'Was that last night, when you talked to him?'

'He said it before, and last night he said it again! I said I felt the Lord was telling me to leave here now and he said, "No, he isn't!" But I feel he is. I don't know what to do about it.'

'Tell John you'll accept his decision,' I suggest, 'if it's still the same after he's fasted and prayed for three days. With any luck, he'll be begging you to leave by lunchtime!'

'That's wicked – I might do it!'

'But how about you, yourself – do you want to leave?'
I ask her.

'I want to be here for these girls, seeing them train to
a high standard, but I worry about my mother. One sug-
gestion is I could be based at Oasis UK and be a
consultant on projects in other parts of the world. So I'm
trying to train up Roshni to take over my role.'

'I met Roshni. She seems happy with the job.'

'Roshni is doing really well. At first, even to go into
high-class boutiques was too hard for her. Now she goes
alone.'

'It's great, what's going on here,' I say, 'seeing people
come up from very poor backgrounds and gain confidence and skills. And it's just as needed in the UK and
wealthier countries, isn't it? People don't have much
faith in themselves, or feel they'll never amount to anything, and need encouragement as much as anybody.
But I'm concerned, recently, about this life-coach
approach to getting people motivated to achieve. It
seems to me it can put more stress on people because it
gets them to look at their lives in isolation, with *me* as the
starting point, and that's not real.'

'I know,' Brenda agrees.

'So what would you say to people who feel stressed
out or inadequate and are looking for inner peace – from
your experience?'

'I'd say to people, "Be open to God,"' Brenda says.
'Our society puts people in a box. And take risks! If God
shows you something, take a risk and do it.'

'You must have felt it was a big risk, leaving everyone
you knew and coming here, not knowing what to
expect?'

'There was such a deep peace inside me when I was
doing what God wanted,' Brenda says, 'and without
that you can't do something so risk-taking. I have felt

very vulnerable, without my family. I've had to be dependent on God. But if anything, I feel safer here than in England.'

The IT trainers come into the office and suggest I go and see their work. A group of young women is seated at the computers, rapt with concentration. Throughout the day, different groups succeed each other, taking advantage of the opportunities for practice and tuition – housewives, older children after school, college students, and the centre's own trainees.

Majella returns from visiting in the community. 'You should be sitting down,' she says firmly. She takes me by the elbow and shepherds me back to the desk on the landing. 'I am going out to buy you juice.'

'How did your visits go?'

'Fine, but the women from the community who wanted to come in and talk to you can't, because it's water day. Water is piped to the slum but it's only switched on once or twice a week; so when word goes round that drinking water's available, the women have to go. But some of the community workers are coming to see you.'

At her insistence, I sit down. I do feel tired. I ask the question that has been in my mind today, perhaps because of my own state. 'Majella, what happens if you offer all these opportunities to women from a poor background but they just don't have the health or stamina to take advantage of it and they can't keep up?'

'That has happened to a few. We work around it,' Majella says. 'You must meet Aditi. When I first met her, she was so weak she could hardly stand up. She had TB and her family were sending her out to work.'

'They sent her out to work, in that state?'

'You need to understand,' Majella says seriously, sitting down and leaning her elbows on the desk, 'that here nobody keeps someone just to feed them.'

I'm ashamed of being judgmental, having no concept of what it's like to risk starvation unless every member of the household goes to work.

'I'm sorry. What did you do for Aditi?'

'We took her to the clinic every day for three years for her medication. She came in here but she was too weak even to sit at the sewing machine, so she would do hand sewing, a few things that she could manage. Then we had a volunteer from the UK who was a designer, and she noticed that Aditi watched her while she was working so she encouraged her and Aditi made some really nice designs. We sold them. Ask her to show you. I'll call her. But I'm bringing you juice first! What flavour do you like – apple or mango?'

Aditi is very thin and very shy. She stands till invited twice to sit down. Majella pats her on the arm encouragingly and settles down to interpret for her.

I ask Aditi how old she is. She is 23, she says. She looks younger than Roshni at 21 and appears much less confident, but when she starts telling her story it's clear that she's a strong character.

'When I was eighteen years old, my mum died,' she starts. 'Till then I didn't know what difficulties were all about. Only when my mum died, we knew what it is to be starving. Mum was in five houses as a domestic worker and she looked after us so well that we never went hungry. When she died, relatives took us to Chennai. My sister is a year younger and my brother is two years younger. I was working in an assembly unit, making files, but I got jaundice and then TB. My father brought me and my brother and sister to Bangalore and we stayed in my father's sister's house. My relatives weren't happy to pay for my keep so they were compelling me to go to work even though I was sick. An Oasis worker visited, and through the community

health check-ups they found out about the TB. I didn't
have a good chance of surviving. Once I even stopped
breathing and they thought I had died.'

'That's when we met Aditi,' Majella says, 'and started
taking her for treatment, and she came to the centre.'

'How long ago was that?'

'I've been here five years now,' Aditi answers. She
adds, 'I'm learning the job well. After I came to Oasis I
was happy. I had a stipend while I was training but my
father fell sick, so the three of us had to take care of my
father, and I was paying for his treatment. My sister
was a housemaid and my brother was a small-time
painter, and it wasn't enough for food. Even now we
have lots of debts. Last year my father died of cancer.
Our grandmother was staying with us and gave a keen
eye to the two girls and found a match for us. My
brother and sister took over all the debts and paid my
wedding expenses, around sixty thousand rupees, and
my mother's eldest sister helped. She has four children
of her own, but she was the only one who supported
us.'

'Tell her about Tanya,' Majella prompts.

'We had a designer called Tanya working in Oasis.'
Aditi's eyes light up. 'It was very interesting to work
with her. I don't mind doing any work; sometimes I even
worked as a maid after going home from work here, but
I liked watching her doing the designs and I got my own
ideas.'

'Do you have any of your designs here?'

Majella gets up. 'I'll see what we have,' she says. She
goes into the workshop and returns with a cellophane
package. Aditi looks slightly embarrassed as Majella
shows a black bag with a curved trim of sequins and
decorative gold stitching shaped as a pocket.

'It's lovely! Really delicate.'

'That's Aditi's style. There were t-shirts as well, and some jewellery, but we sold them all,' Majella says.

I'm not surprised. Aditi obviously does have a flair for it; it's tempting for first-timers to pile on the decorations but this is effective for being understated.

Aditi returns to the subject of her marriage. 'My husband is a carpenter, called Joseph,' she says, with a huge smile.

'Did you know him before you married, if it was arranged by your grandmother?' I ask her.

'This boy was a neighbour and I knew him before we got married, but I didn't know he liked me.' Another wide smile.

Majella turns and asks Aditi something, then tells me, 'I'm asking if I can tell you about her wedding day.'

Aditi laughs.

'On the day of Aditi's wedding, all the Oasis staff went,' Majella recalls. 'The church wedding was at 4 o'clock and we were all there by 3.45. The bridegroom was there but the bride was not there!

'At 4.30 Aditi arrives and runs down the aisle in her beautiful sari, like the Runaway Bride in the film, you know! It was so sad – she was late because she didn't have anyone to bring her to the church.' Aditi takes up the story here, with Majella translating. 'I had to get ready, with no mother, and I couldn't get a rickshaw. The boy was standing waiting for me. The priest had another wedding afterwards and he gave me a mouthful, and then after that he told us to say our vows!'

She laughs and goes on, 'I came back to work here after the marriage. I work here now in packing and I do hand-embroidery, sewing on the machine, shopping – everything! When I was working with Tanya, I gave her ideas but I didn't know it would take off. But Tanya was happy with it and gave me a certificate.'

'How did it feel, when you realised you had a talent for design?'

'I felt, "I can do it!" I had never had that confidence.'

'Has it stayed with you, that confidence?'

'Sometimes I have a fear within me,' Aditi admits, 'but I feel I can do lots of things now – bag design and bangles and patterns.'

'What would you say to people, Aditi, who don't have that confidence and feel they can't do anything much in their life?'

Her answer is certainly confident. 'I would say to people, "When God has been with me and has made so many changes in me, he will make changes in your life as well." I thought many times, "Is this my fate? Is this all, in my life?" But now I have the strength to deal with anything that comes my way. I have hope: still more will happen to me. Every time I believe and I pray, I get what I want. Now I am receiving prosperity, I want others to ask God and receive their prosperity.'

I remind myself here that for Aditi prosperity means having the health to work and enough to eat. This is not the 'prosperity gospel' preached by some evangelists, asking God to pile ever more blessings on top of personal (material) advantages for the person who asks for them. It's knowing she has enough to survive, being thankful that life has ceased to be nothing but sickness and destitution, and wanting the same for others.

'I have spoken to my brother and sister,' Aditi says, 'and said to them, "Don't think it's difficult all the time; trust God and you won't even know it's difficulties you're going through."'

'Do you have a dream, for the future?' I ask Aditi.

'I do have a dream,' she says. 'I read the word of God and I pray, and I have a desire to know God more.'

The meeting in the office continues after lunch, and as the afternoon progresses there is a constant migration of people up and down the stairs. It's the end of the working week, which means all the staff return to base for the Friday prayer meeting.

Majella comes and rejoins me on the landing. It's the first opportunity I've had to ask her a little about herself.

'I'm a pastor's wife,' she says, pulling a comical face. 'I don't fit the bill, I know; I'm too loud! In the beginning I tried so hard to be like everyone expected a pastor's wife to be, but now I give up; I just have to be myself.'

'There are probably people who talk to you because you are you,' I suggest, 'who would never come near you if you were meek and mild.'

'Some people have said that they never would talk to me if I'd been like a pastor's wife,' Majella agrees, but still she gives an involuntary sigh.

Two older women, both slum dwellers now employed by Oasis, have come in. Geeta and Daisy work together and take turns in speaking. Daisy laughs more readily. Geeta looks the kind of person anyone would turn to in a crisis; there is a steadiness about her and a sense of having seen suffering, her own and everyone else's.

'We are tutors in community health development,' Geeta explains. 'It's a new job. We enjoy serving these people. They are very depressed and lost and we are helping them to get hope.'

'What's it like working in the community as well as living there?' I ask them. 'Are you more acceptable to the people because you're one of them, or are they less likely to accept what you say?'

'They didn't trust us at all at first,' Geeta says.

'People used to ignore us,' agrees Daisy. 'One person told another not to let us in.'

'But we didn't give up,' Geeta says firmly.

They come across as people who don't give up.

'The first self-help group was eight ladies,' Daisy says. 'Now there are fourteen groups in the Women's Federation with nearly two hundred members overall.'

'Is it run on the same lines as the women's groups in Mumbai?'

'The same model is used here,' Daisy affirms.

'As well,' Geeta adds, 'each group sets its own rules, such as prompt attendance and neat appearance at meetings, and as well as the savings scheme there is help with health care, counselling and education.'

'How did your acceptance in the community grow from people not letting you in the door to setting up all these groups?' I ask them.

'We live in the community so they see how we live,' Geeta says simply.

That's a real commitment. This work isn't easy for any of the workers but it has to be easier to work selflessly for eight or more hours a day then go home somewhere else. Living life in full view of the people you're working with is a 24/7 job.

'We see a lot of changes in the community,' Daisy says. 'People used to cheat each other, take money from each other, have affairs with many men.'

'Many of the husbands drink,' Geeta says, 'but they are aware of us. They see us and trust us and begin to trust each other. We feel so close now; they are like family.'

I meet two more community workers, Latha and Bethesda, but there's little time to talk; the prayer meeting is about to begin.

Chapter 17

Sailing Through Storms

The computer room is crowded with people, on chairs, on the floor, standing in the doorways and on the balcony. Once the prayer starts, there's a sense of everyone letting go of weariness and busyness and becoming still. We sing – in English – and people pray. The atmosphere is both relaxed and reverent and I'm struck by everyone's focus. This is not something separate from work; it's the reason and motive for what they do all week.

John is asked to speak, and talks about a time when he and his brother Andrew were caught in a storm while sailing up the west coast of Scotland. They realised that, experienced sailors though they both were, this was beyond their capabilities. Their mother – my sister-in-law – who is tiny, was in the hold, unable to contribute any physical strength to her sons' struggle with the elements but praying with every fibre of faith she possessed. John likens this to the work of Oasis India – an undertaking beyond the human strength and capacities of all the staff, yet made possible by the power of God.

There is silence when he finishes.

We say goodbye to the staff and I thank Majella especially for her care today, and take a rickshaw to the centre of Bangalore. It's an effort to stay awake. John is still trying to work at the airport, making notes on the meeting

while it's still fresh in his mind. The day has been productive, he says. It has been for me as well, despite having to cancel the original plan of visiting families in the
slum. I wouldn't have wanted to miss meeting any of the
people I met today. I have a feeling they will stay with me
for a long time.

I hadn't fully taken account of how much more
relaxed Bangalore felt, compared with Mumbai, though
I noticed there was more of a breeze, the buildings were
less tightly packed and palm trees punctuated the horizon. Also, while we were there, my legs were much less
swollen. Flying into Mumbai again, the intensity of the
atmosphere is striking, even at this time of night. We
take a taxi to the office and John drives the car home. I
hope he's awake but I'm too sleepy myself to worry.
What jolts me awake is what I see when we drive along
a major stretch of dual carriageway and round a bend
under a flyover. There are people lying in the road,
asleep.

Not *by* the road. *In* the road. The traffic is missing
them by centimetres – swerving at the last minute to
avoid colliding with their heads, not their feet. These
sleepers are lying with their feet overhanging the edge
of the road and their heads facing the traffic.

'Why don't they choose somewhere safer to sleep?' I
am horrified.

John nods towards the central reservation, a thin strip
of raised concrete. 'A lot of people sleep there for safety,'
he says. There's an almost unbroken line of people
asleep, some wrapped in a blanket, some just in their
clothes, with bare feet. A few are walking around. All
along the roadsides, too, are people asleep. The ones
lying in the road have not been able to find somewhere
safer. Perhaps they consider it preferable, if they're
going to get run over, that a vehicle crushes their head

and kills them outright rather than crushes their legs and feet and leaves them unable to work. How would I know? I have no idea what goes through the mind of someone who decides their best chance is to sleep in the road.

* * * *

It's Saturday morning. I wake to weekend sounds of children – watching *Balamory* again – and over breakfast John says we are going into Bombay, to the 'nice part' – the port area with the imposing old buildings. 'You've been here ten days and all I've shown you is slums!'

We pile into the car and drive for two hours through the traffic to uptown Mumbai, the site of the old colonial quarters, the Gateway To India arch, a wide plaza and an enormously grand hotel which John waves me into: 'If you have to keep going to the loo then go for the best!'

The port, with all the ocean-going ships and the lines of moored boats offshore, somehow gives me a sense of the vastness of India. It's a world away from the cosy scale of the British coast. In the shopping streets, we are repeatedly approached by beggars. 'Most of these are professional beggars,' Charmaine says. 'If you give to one, all the others will come round you. Only a few are street children.' She looks straight ahead as some clamour for money, and only turns towards a few ragged children, and I follow her discernment.

When sightseeing is done and our own family is buying drinks and ice creams from a kiosk, a boy appears and holds out a grubby hand, without much hope. 'No,' Charmaine says, in English, 'but if you're thirsty I'll get you a drink.' He nods and she invites him to choose. The children have bottles of water and mini-Cornetto ice creams. The boy stands next to them and makes no decision. I think he likes standing with them, like one of a family. Charmaine suggests a bottle of Pepsi and he nods.

'Shall I get him something to eat?' I ask and she says, 'Yes, you can but there are only biscuits. You want biscuits?' she asks him. He looks up at the shelf where packs of plain biscuits are stacked, and nods again, but his eyes slide downwards and sideways towards the ice cream cabinet. It's a speaking glance that makes us laugh.

'You want ice cream instead?' Charmaine asks and his head dips very slightly, an almost-nod, as if not quite believing the option. 'Which one? This kind or this one, or this?' Charmaine asks him but he is motionless and speechless. 'My children are having these,' she helps him out.

Again, the tiniest movement of the head. His face is expressionless and his body is tense. I'm not sure why. Does he think it's not going to happen so there's no point making a choice?

'Chocolate or vanilla?' Charmaine asks, but the child is turned to stone. 'Chocolate,' she tells the vendor. She hands the cone to the boy who takes it from her but doesn't move. 'It's yours,' she tells him. 'You can eat it.'

Very slowly he peels back a strip of wrapper. He backs away from us a few steps and looks at us, wary like a wild animal. I'm not sure what the problem is. Charmaine waves her hand at him. 'Bye bye!'

She speaks briskly and I'm taken aback; it seems out of character for her to dismiss the child like this. But the effect it has is instant. The boy's face lights up, and he springs into action; he takes a huge bite of his ice cream, gives us a radiant smile and strides away confidently. I realise, with a lurch, that he was waiting to see what was wanted of him. What does he have to do usually, in return for ice cream? By sending him on his way, Charmaine has let him know the gift is free.

On the way home we stop in a part of town where, looking down from a road bridge, Charmaine shows me a vast area of what look like concrete cattle stalls with line after line of washing hung up above them. 'These are the *ghats*,' she says, 'where the washing is done by the *dhobis*. See, in those vats of water, the dhobis treading the clothes with their feet?' It's a hive of industry, a whole world of private lives trodden spotless by strangers and hung out in public to dry, before being delivered back to their owners.

Back home, everyone takes a nap before preparing dinner for this evening's visitor, a businessman who has met John before and is considering donating to the work of Oasis. The cool shower is relaxing, after the heat and grime of Mumbai and the pace of the last ten days. I lather up the shampoo and, covered in suds from head to toe, step into the flow of water. Abruptly, it stops flowing. *Oh. No.* Unscheduled water cuts have been occurring increasingly. The last time it happened in the evening the water stayed off till next morning. *Why does it have to happen now?*

It won't even gain any ticks on my list of conquered fears. Even nightmares never presented a fear of being marooned in a bathroom, naked apart from a soap-sud veneer, when a stranger rings at the door with a potential major donation to charity hanging in the balance. I remember the tap in the wall by the toilet. Wiping lather out of my eyes, I grab the bucket. Enough water is left in the pipe to half fill it. I kneel down and rinse my hair in the bucket, then tip it up gingerly and ration out the water over my body.

My clothes still stick to me but it's better than nothing. And it gives me a sudden sharp insight into the lives of some families here, washing their faces, their teeth and their babies in a bucket of water by the roadside.

The businessman, over dinner, professes himself impressed by Oasis' projects and leaves promising a donation of twenty thousand pounds to expand the provision of IT education for the disadvantaged.

This really is 'good news for the poor' and John and Charmaine are delighted.

Except that the promise never materialises.

And, as always, it is the poor who lose out.

Chapter 18

Finding Oasis

I didn't go to India looking for a spiritual experience, only visiting family and meeting people, but it turned out to be a spiritual journey. The love of God, like a magnet, draws in people who thirst for love and never expected to find it.

Some of the people I met had been deprived of everything that spells security: income, choice, family, safety . . . Others had those securities but voluntarily sacrificed them for the sake of empowering the powerless.

I asked the same questions of street people, prostitutes, AIDS survivors, slum dwellers and charity workers who had come through severe sufferings – their own and others' – with their faith alive. The questions were: 'What was the worst?', 'What helped you survive?', 'Do you have a dream?' and 'What do you have to teach us?'

The answers, like the people, were individual. Everyone was searching for an oasis: that resource of peace where their basic needs would be met and their inner self restored. They didn't know if it was possible to find it. But they certainly knew when they did. The route to the oasis, however, was not so individual. The same words kept recurring: love, acceptance, trust, prayer – and Jesus Christ.

Prayer seemed to be the highway to God; many people referred to times when impossible things happened,

closed doors opened, confidence blossomed or guidance
was given, as a result of prayer. And it happened for me.
The highway of prayer started out in the heart of the
individual, but it opened out when it became a shared
highway.

The current emphasis among lifestyle gurus – both
Eastern and Western varieties – on 'finding your own
path' seemed to me to be a diversion from that highway
to God. If everyone thinks the highway belongs to them
and they're free to use it to go in any direction, the out-
come is not peace but pile-ups.

The path painfully and devotedly carved out by Jesus
Christ is a narrow highway but a well-trodden one and,
as more people take it, it shines in the dark. People are
afraid of getting lost in the crowd, their needs unmet,
their individuality submerged. I experienced that fear
when stranded in Mumbai, and the poor and ignored
live with it every day. But stepping into the life of Jesus,
the light of the world, means not being lost and never
going unseen.

God is not asking people to give things up or saying,
'Thou shalt not have . . .' but only saying, 'Let me save
you from false securities and hidden agendas – your
own and each other's – and free you to trust in the One
who will never let you down.' It doesn't solve the problem of suffering or make life stress-free. But for many of
the people I met it had turned suffering into something
so productive they were even willing to take on others'
as well – like choosing to go on living in the slum when
they could move on and up.

For them, the oasis wasn't a place of beauty, or even
clean. It didn't meet their every need. It wasn't a feel-
good experience. But from every viewpoint they met the
eyes of Jesus, in unlikely places and in unlovely people.
They were still living in the desert. But, impossibly, the

202 *Finding Oasis*

desert bloomed and the elusive oasis was found, right where they stood.

Thank you for keeping me company on this part of my journey, and may God send you good companions for the next stage of yours.

– to be continued

The author's royalties from this book will be donated to the work of Oasis India. If you would like to donate, connect to the Oasis Trust website www.oasisuk.org, click the Donate Now button and specify Oasis India. More information is available from www.oasisindia.org

* * * *

author's website: http://clarenonhebel.com

Endnotes

1 The local language of Mumbai.
2 About £1.80.
3 The drop-in centre for street children.
4 Uttar Pradesh.
5 The home for women and children with HIV.
6 About £5,000.
7 A nursery.
8 The state-run children's home.
9 Food offered to Hindu gods.